teens @ the library series

Hold them in your heart

Successful

Strategies

for Library

Services to

At-Risk Teens

JoAnn G. Mondowney

Neal-Schuman Publishers, Inc.

New York ALAMEDA FREE LIBRARY   London

Published by Neal-Schuman Publishers, Inc.
100 Varick Street
New York, NY 10013

The paper used in this publication meets the minimum requirements of American National Standard for Information Sciences—Permanence of Paper for Printed Library Materials, ANSI Z39.48–1992.∞

This publication was supported in whole or in part by the U.S. Department of Education under the provisions of the Library Services and Construction Act, administered in California by the State Librarian.

Library of Congress Cataloging-in-Publication Data

Mondowney, JoAnn G.
    Hold them in your heart : successful strategies for library services to at-risk teens / JoAnn G. Mondowney.
       p. cm. — (teens @ the library)
    ISBN 1-55570-393-3 (alk. paper)
    1. Public libraries—Services to teenagers—United States. 2. Public Libraries—Services to the poor—United States. 3. Public libraries—Services to minorities—United States. 4. Libraries and the poor—United States. 5. Libraries and minorities—United States. 6. Young adults' libraries—United States. I. Title. II. Series.

Z718.5 .M57 2001
027.62'6—dc21

00-058413

Contents

List of Figures

Foreword

Those of us who work with teenagers in libraries have many reasons to celebrate. The young adults we meet and work with on a daily basis give us great hope for the future. The teenage population is growing at an unprecedented rate. The world seems to be taking notice of them as never before, as evidenced by recent cover stories in the major national news magazines. Teens are now a prime target group for merchandizing campaigns because their spending power is growing prodigiously.

Today's teens face so many difficult choices. Decisions are clouded by conflicting information, competing needs, and unrealized potential. While the developmental tasks teens face remain timeless, the means of acquiring the skills necessary to achieve those tasks are too often out of reach or unavailable. The library can help meet the increasingly sophisticated information needs of today's teens. I'm proud to serve as the editor of and to introduce a new series of books called *teens @ the library* which will offer librarians and teachers high quality, practical, up-to-date guidance in planning and implementing to excellent service for young adults in their libraries.

Margaret Edwards, whom I call the patron saint of young adult librarianship, wrote in her classic book *The Fair Garden and the Swarm of Beasts: The Library and the Young Adult*[1] that, "There is no age group more important than the young adults, who in a few short years will be guiding the destiny of this nation, deciding among other things whether to drop the bomb or to use atomic energy for man's good. Fortunately they are impressionable, more open to ideas, more ready to listen to suggestions than are adults, and they are more likely to become thoughtful readers" (Edwards, 1994).

Unfortunately, for a variety of reasons that books in the *teens @ the library* series will address, young adults get too little respect in our libraries. The Young Adult Library Association's (YALSA's) training program is called "Serving the Underserved" for good reasons. Teenagers are routinely left out in terms of library collection development, specialized training for staff, young adult specialist positions, budgeting, programming, employment, outreach, etc. Teens are not well served on a personal, individual basis nor in terms of how their intellectual, emotional, physical, and psychological needs are met. The public and school libraries that ought to be teens' safe haven and information central instead are too often YA desolation zones that erect roadblocks (both inadvertent and intentional) that keep too many teens out and drive too many others away.

The media pays less attention to one segment of the teen population, those who are "at risk," than they do to high-achieving teen athletes, computer whizzes, and scholars. Delinquency, substance abuse, teen pregnancy, school failure, homelessness, and poverty continue to degrade the lives and limit the potential of far too many young people. The books in this series take the view that libraries and librarians, working in the context of their communities, can make a significant positive impact on the lives of teens and—indeed, I believe they must do so. If our teens are at risk, our society is at risk. If our teens are not library aware, our libraries, too, are at risk.

This book, *Hold Them in Your Heart: Successful Strategies for Library Services to At-Risk Teens*, is a very appropriate first book in the series. Its author, JoAnn Mondowney, clearly lays out the reasons that special attention must be paid to the growing numbers of teens who are in one way or another "at risk" in our society. Mondowney encapsulates the valuable lessons learned during the implementation of the San Francisco Bay Area Models of serving this population of youth. She then specifies tested strategies for gaining support for an at-risk initiative both within the library and in the critically important greater community. Her outstanding chapter about conducting a needs assessment puts this important data-collecting technique within the reach of anyone, in any sized organization, and explains why every library should conduct such assessments.

Planning and evaluation go hand-in-hand, as accountability is necessary in any successful program. While Mondowney suggests that even modest efforts in serving at-risk teens can pay off in big ways for many communities, she also provides useful guidance about the process of applying for and obtaining grants and testing other funding sources for the financial support necessary to create and implement larger-scaled efforts. Other program models "Beyond the Bay" are also cited, and an extensive bibliography and an appendix listing youth-serving organizations, complete this inspiring and useful book.

When I read the manuscript for *Hold Them in Your Heart* I was extremely pleased that it filled all the criteria that I and the Neal-Schuman editorial team established for the series. Specifically, it and the books which will follow:

- Address the needs of youth-serving librarians in both public and school libraries,
- Draw from the best, most current research,
- Target the needs of today's changing teenage population,
- Cite the most innovative models,
- Provide practical suggestions, that have been real-world-tested, and
- Call on each of us to realize the highest ideals of our profession.

The next two books in the series will be:

1) *Do It Right! Best Practices for Serving Young Adults in School and Public Libraries.* Co-authors Patrick Jones and Joel Shoemaker show how to apply the best customer service theory and techniques to serving young adults in libraries. Shoemaker explores ways to provide the best possible customer service techniques in school library settings and Jones offers tips and techniques for turning teenagers into "raving fans" of the public library.
2) *Booktalking That Works.* Noted booktalker Jennifer Bromann offers proven techniques for booktalking to today's teens who have grown up with the Internet, digital television, and Walkmans. She offers step-by-step guidance as well as 50+ successful booktalks.

Librarians who work with teens generally have a sense of mission about their work. "Libraries Change Lives" is not just an American Library Association National Library Week slogan but a call to take up the challenge and serve the underserved. Caring and professional service by librarians might make the critical difference between failure and success in the lives of today's teens.

You know there are *teens @ the library*. Take the first step. Make a difference, one teen at a time.

Joel Shoemaker
September 2000

NOTE

1. Edwards, Margaret A., *The Fair Garden and the Swarm of Beasts: The Library and the Young Adult*. Chicago: American Library Association, 1994. Reprint.

Preface

Millions of children are "at-risk" in the United States today. The term "at-risk" is not a new one; the medical field has used it for years to denote an individual who has a greater chance than others of incurring a specific health problem or disease. It is now most commonly used to describe social phenomena: at-risk teens. Using commonly accepted estimates and this definition, our libraries have the opportunity to serve 15 million young people who have a diminished chance of succeeding in life unless we devise programs and services to help them. This is a worthy challenge.

These young people, whose daily lives include poverty, but also drug use, crime, and violence, have a very poor chance of growing up to lead successful, productive lives. Delinquency, substance abuse, and teen pregnancy are likely to contribute to failure in school and failure in society. Fortunately, libraries are in an excellent position to help teenagers who otherwise would probably not develop the skills they need to succeed. In some communities, libraries may be the only organizations that reach out to members of this group who do not attend school.

Developing library services that will meet the needs of this special population is not easy because often the librarian responsible for serving at-risk youth has little or no support system. The book you are holding now was developed to provide critical information to assist in developing successful programs. This is an updated and expanded version of a wonderful manual originally developed by the San Francisco Bay Area Youth-At-Risk Project. The Bay Area Library and Information System supported development of this book in order to communicate proven strategies for serving this vulnerable population to a broader audience.

To serve at-risk youth, librarians need to understand how to become effective, visible advocates for preteens and teenagers. They have to be able to collaborate productively with other groups in the community, analyze data, and learn basic grant-writing skills. *Hold Them in Your Heart: Successful Strategies for Library Services to At-Risk Teens* provides the basic information needed to assess community needs in this area and design services for meeting those needs. This guide also includes detailed to-do lists, planning templates, and descriptions of sample projects that the author and program developers have used in setting up successful programs for at-risk teens.

The details of the comprehensive San Francisco Bay Area Youth-At-Risk project illustrate various methods further serving this vulnerable population, and highlights from exemplary at-risk programs nationwide further demonstrate the case for caring for these teenagers and thinking creatively about enhancing programs for them in your library service area.

Hold Them in Your Heart: Successful Strategies for Library Services to At-Risk Teens has an introduction and seven chapters. The Introduction presents some of the problems that today's youth face and the author's personal experiences in reaching out to at-risk teenagers. Chapter 1, "Lessons Learned: Making the Case for Library Services to At-Risk Youth," presents the needs, characteristics, and developmental stages of teenagers along with current information on serving them. Chapter 2, "Public Library Services for Youth-At-Risk: The San Francisco Bay Area Models" describes this comprehensive and ambitious outreach project in which nine libraries developed outstanding programs for at-risk youth ages 12 to 18. Chapter 3, "Strategies for Gaining Support" explains how to gain the necessary support for services from community members, library administrators, and staff. Chapter 4, "Conducting a Youth Needs Assessment," presents step-by-step activities for conducting the all-important needs assessment. Chapter 5, "Are We There Yet? Planning and Evaluation," explains how to plan and evaluate a project, featuring plans developed by the Bay Area Youth-at-Risk libraries. This chapter stresses the importance of a meaningful and useful evaluation process. Chapter 6, "Money Talk: Obtaining the Grants and Gifts That Make These Projects Viable," provides basic proposal writing tips and includes funding sources and sample proposals. Chapter 7, "Beyond the Bay: Other Model Programs," highlights innovative library programs nationwide. Suggestions for a number of inexpensive, creative "starter projects" complete the chapter. The appendix provides sample promotional materials that can be adapted to specific programs.

The title—*Hold Them in Your Heart: Strategies for Library Services to At-Risk Teens*—is a reminder that caring is an essential component of effective library services for youth. Even the best-designed, best-funded program in the world cannot effectively serve the needs of these young people unless it fosters caring relationships in a caring environment.

Introduction

My name is Tenetia and I am 16 years old. I have a nine-month-old daughter. My mother's boyfriend is the baby's father. I am out of school and depend on welfare for support. I wish there was a program that would help me finish school and help me with daycare for my daughter.
—From Advocates for Children and Youth Project

In 1982, educators and social workers defined the term "at-risk" as "adolescents whose potential of becoming healthy and productive adults is reduced because they are at high risk of encountering serious problems at home, in school, or in their communities."[1] Further defined, the term includes youth between the ages of 12 and 18 who experience school failure, poor health outcomes, racial discrimination, family dysfunction, delinquency, poverty, and unemployment.[2] Typically, large numbers of at-risk youth such as Tenetia, the young woman quoted above, face severe emotional and psychological pressures that destroy or limit their ability to survive in a complex and hostile world.

One may well argue that all teenagers in America are to a greater or lesser degree "at-risk." They are the only group in the United States whose death rate has increased in the last 20 years (accidents, suicide, and homicide). Then again, one could say that all of society is at-risk, with crime and drugs exacting extraordinary amounts of grief and pain on a daily basis in almost every part of this country. Currently however, there are millions of young people across the nation growing up more at-risk than other youth in our society. They are extremely vulnerable to drug addiction, alcohol abuse, teen pregnancy, suicide, and multiple sources of hopelessness. They live in "severely distressed neighborhoods—places that, according to the Annie Casey Foundation, have high levels of four or more of the following risk factors: poverty, female-headed families, high school dropouts, unemployment, and reliance on welfare."[3]

General Colin Powell, chair of America's Promise notes that " . . . most of our young people are doing well. They are growing up in solid families. They see success ahead, but the reality of life in America is also that there are [millions] of young people who are not on that road to success, who are not yet living their dream. . . . We need to do a better job of sharing, a better job of reaching down, back and across; of helping young people who have many kinds of needs. They are our hope. They are our future. And guess what? They're also our present, and we have to deal with them in the present."[4]

In addition to those at the highest risk, over five million young people of the "working poor" are at-risk of not reaching their potential.[5] Study after study confirms the connection between living in poverty and "suffering a host of lousy developmental, educational, and adult outcomes."[6] "Young people from poor families are most likely to live in unsafe neighborhoods and to be unsupervised during after school hours. These young people are also the least likely to have access to constructive alternatives. They are at extremely high risk; they are the youth whose lives hang in the balance."[7]

Fortunately, many of the adults who see these young people become concerned and develop a strong desire to intervene and help improve their quality of life. The task force from the Council on Adolescent Development that wrote *A Matter of Time: Risk and Opportunities in the Non-School Hours* reported that while many public agencies serving youth concentrated on treatment or remediation rather than development, public libraries have been an exception. But although libraries have a different focus, they still have far to go before they can claim success in serving at-risk youth. "If libraries are to serve youth better, they must develop thoughtful and responsive policies and programs to address the unmet needs of young adolescents. Further, libraries should help focus community attention on the welfare of children and serve as active sources of information on existing community programs for children, youth, and families."[8]

For many libraries located in at-risk communities, accepting responsibility for providing services is not the issue. The problem appears to be how to minimize the psychological distance and cultural divide between library staff and the at-risk youth so that library resources can make a real difference in the lives of these young people.

Today, more than ever, it is critical for libraries to play a supporting role in assisting at-risk youth, even if the contribution is very modest. Fortunately, we do not have to reinvent the wheel. We can look to and learn from the lasting legacy of the California Bay Area Youth-at-Risk

Project, which was funded in 1988, with implementation beginning in 1990. This project raised the consciousness level of many librarians and provided a blueprint to follow in the delivery of services to youth at-risk. This extensive effort proved that "libraries are an invaluable resource for teenagers and librarians need to be more actively involved in responding to the needs of at-risk youth."[9]

It is not necessary to have enormous grants, although they always help. If you have limited funding and staff, yet want to lessen the psychological distance between many youth and your library, you will still find several inexpensive, interesting, and easy-to-implement activities. An indispensable part of finding a way to these teenagers is caring, which brings us back to the title: *Hold Them in Your Heart*. I offer the following story from my own experience as an example.

When I first started working as a young adult librarian, more often than not my state of mind was, "take this job and shove it, I ain't workin' here no more." I felt unprepared to work with unmotivated, disinterested, and unruly young people in a library setting. My training was by far more suitable for "library ready" young people, those who wanted reader's advisory, homework assistance, or a quiet place to study.

However, I was dealing with an entirely different population. Rarely would anyone request a book from the extensive teen reading list. Nevertheless, I was always ready to booktalk the likes of *The Diary of Anne Frank, Death Be Not Proud,* or *All Quiet on the Western Front*. But, if I suggested a book to read I was met with looks and responses ranging from "thank you, no" to "are you crazy?" All too frequently after I had located the information needed for school assignments, many of the teens would point at the page and ask [do I] "start here, [and] stop there?" They were content to simply copy whatever I outlined on the page for them. And the noise—to this day I can summon the noise level, which was more like a crowded recreation center than a library.

Instead of writing a traditional report, I wrote a poem for my first annual report at the Pennsylvania Avenue Branch of the Enoch Pratt Free Library in Baltimore, Maryland. It expresses my sentiments during those trying times.

What happened to the lady that was here last year?
What happened to the lady that was here year before last?
What happened to—listen they are in the past.
Well who are you?
I'm the new young adult librarian.
Oh yeah, my name is Wine, me and my friends come in all the time.

Really, so you like to read?
Are you crazy, reading ain't my speed.
Well, why come here to spend your time?
To sit in the Y-Corner and organize crime!
Hey Miss, y'all got any love stories?
Sure, there's *Mr. & Mrs., Bo Jo Jones*.
Nah, I saw it on TV.
Try the book. Nah, the movie was good enough for me.
Okay, We have *My Darling, My Hamburger*.
My darling, my what? All right, let me see what that's about.
Oh, I'm sorry, all of our copies are out.
You got any karate books left?
No.
Why?
You ever heard of theft?
We want to see a sex book.
I want to know about drugs.
Tell the guard I want to look.
This library ain't got nothin.
What do you mean?
Well take a look.
There ain't many good books.
You try to be what's happenin' now, but you ain't even got no sounds.
And whether you know it or not, I might mention—
Sometime we come here for a little attention.
I'm not going to go on.
Besides there's not a person you can trust in this place.
Why?
'Cause every few months there's a brand new face.

But this was only one experience. My most challenging—and reward-ing—experiences in providing library services to at-risk youth occurred over a six-year period at the Hollins-Payson Branch of the Enoch Pratt Library, referred to simply as Branch 2. I began working there as a young adult librarian and later served for five years as the branch manager. For-tunately, in between working at the Pennsylvania Avenue Branch and being assigned to Branch 2, I had taken time off to get a library degree. So I was somewhat better prepared to take on the challenge.

Part of Pratt's folklore included several "while working at Hollins-Payson" horror stories and tales of woe. This was 1971, and staff system-wide shared Branch 2 stories, seemingly to console or congratulate one another for surviving. Hearing someone else's horror tale seemed to minimize your own troubled circumstances if you happened to work in a sometimes difficult and taxing setting. A tale of woe affirmed your good fortune if you worked at a nice traditional library. For many, the infamous Branch 2 was the last place they would ever want to work. On the morning in 1973 when I learned that I had been assigned as a young adult librarian to Hollins-Payson, I took the rest of the day off and seriously considered never returning to the Pratt Library.

The Hollins-Payson community had the city's highest rates of so many negative things: homicide, vandalism, unemployment, high school dropouts, drug use, child abuse, teen pregnancy, and juvenile delinquency. In short, an enormous proportion of the community's members was at-risk. Many whites feared coming to the library because it was located in the predominately African-American section of the community. At night, African Americans were afraid to go to certain stores and carryout restaurants located in the mostly white section. Racial tensions between African Americans and whites in the community certainly affected library use. Staff served a complex and chaotic community, whose traumatic experiences and ways of life we did not always understand. Frequently we provided information for crises—the effects of lead poisoning, illegal drug identification, abortion, pregnancy, arrest, and the like. In addition, as an integral part of the community, we suffered our share of verbal abuse, vandalism, burglaries, and undisciplined behavior.

Getting young adults to visit the library was no problem. In fact, there were times when we could not even seat everyone who came in. Why? There was literally nowhere else to go. The neighborhood had nothing open at night—no theaters, no bowling alleys—just a library. Since many teens used the library as the checkpoint and local hangout, the challenge was getting them to participate in library-related activities. With mutual support, stamina, dedication, commitment, and cooperation from each staff member, we managed to survive to provide excellent service and creative programming for our young adults. We nurtured those who reached out for attention and understanding on a daily basis. Eventually, the changes in Branch 2 were almost miraculous. It definitely went from worst to first in effective outreach and meaningful programming. For many community residents it became a refreshing source of hope—an oasis in the middle of a dry desolate desert.

Some excerpts from the June 1975 Annual Report—this time more than a poem—illustrate part of the process.

For the first few months at Branch 2, the library was dominated by teenagers who used the library for socializing, magazine browsing, and school assignments in that order. Occasionally someone would ask about a book for pleasure. Usually they wanted a paperback that had been checked out in a back pocket or a notebook. A very small number of white teenagers used the library, usually accompanied by a parent who asked for whatever the teen needed. They always looked frightened or uncomfortable. The small number of African-American teenagers who used the library and read extensively also appeared uncomfortable. During those early months, I was confronted constantly by the "regulars" who demanded to find out "where I was coming from." I think I passed the test by being consistent in my responses, that I was there for them, to listen, to help if I could. At first it was disheartening to hear some of the teens accuse me of being "phony" when I asked among other questions:

1.   Do you like to read?
2.   What types of programs would you like to have in the library?
3.   Have you read a book recently?
4.   What do you plan to do with your life?

Most of the teens answered these questions, although they sometimes gave phony, smart-alecky answers. From talking with the teenagers, I concluded that many of them had a preconceived notion that most adults are "plastic beings." Consequently, aside from not being accustomed to honestly expressing their ideas, hopes, and fears with adults, they didn't really care to share.

Most troubling however, was the fact that the majority of the teens consistently said they did not like to read. Later, I learned many of them disliked reading because of their limited skills. Several of the teens read as children, and a few read more than they cared to discuss. Therefore, for fear of being labeled insane, I did not wage an open campaign in the name of reading (e.g., waving a book each time I saw a teen). To entice teens to read, I waged a subtle campaign. I spruced up the Young Adult Corner a little. The Young Adult book collection was small, which made it difficult to fill in empty spaces and create book displays. On the table that housed their favorite magazines I placed books and booklists that would be of interest to them. The talkative regulars frequently complained because I was usually reading when they wanted to talk. This always gave me the opportunity to discuss the book I was reading or to discuss a book

I had recently read. My reading campaign gradually became less subtle. There were many sporadic readers and a few consistent ones. I made progress with some of the nonreaders. They at least respected the fact that I loved to read. I could also carry on a serious conversation about books without being labeled "phony."

Asking young adults for ideas about meaningful programs proved futile. My suggestions such as films, speakers, and clubs received negative responses. No suggestion appeared "hip" enough. Their suggestions were inappropriate for a library. In all sincerity, they wanted to have dances and parties with red lights, without chaperones, from 9:00 p.m. until. . . . Of course, they wanted to bring food, alcoholic beverages, and "reefer." This was considered "hip." In November [1973], the dance contest "Spend the Evening Truckin' " was attended by 75 enthusiastic, but nearly impossible to discipline, teens. I awarded prizes to the first, second, and third place contest winners. I won over quite a few young adults by having the contest, and I will always remain appreciative of the staff who supported me in my endeavor.

Not long ago, I saw two former teens I knew when I served as the branch manager at Hollins-Payson. Tony tracked me down and thanked me for making a difference in his life. He was 32 years old at the time, with two children, and proud to say with book in hand, "I am still reading." I happened upon Pam while she was shopping for her 17-year-old daughter, who was about to graduate from high school. Pam became teary eyed as she shared with her daughter the good times everybody had at the library and remembered attending many of the "fun" programs. Tony and Pam told me about former teen "regulars," mostly young men who were either dead, in jail, or selling and using drugs. Sadly, those teens had not become productive adults. But it was still encouraging to hear positive news—Peanut has become a building engineer for a company in downtown Baltimore, and Pam's sister Sharon was doing okay; Missy was doing well with two children. I am convinced that the library and staff played a significant role in enhancing the quality of life for a great number of young people at the Hollins-Payson Library. Unfortunately, often you do not realize the effect that you have on someone until much later, if at all.

The task of providing consistent, meaningful, quality library service to an at-risk population can be very difficult. Your best efforts can by eclipsed by sheer volume. Yet, you must not remain overwhelmed or discouraged. You may begin by determining to make a difference for one teen at a time. If you take the challenge, trust me, it will serve you well. I know I learned a lot about suffering, despair, resiliency, and what is most important in life from the young people at Branch 2. Not only did they bring out the very best creative leadership and managerial skills I had, they humbled me for life. I learned that the capacity to work with teens at-risk requires empathy, insight, sensitivity, compassion, patience, and lots of communication. In other words, work with this group is difficult, often thankless, and has few short-term rewards. However, your greatest chance of success in reaching these teens lies in using numerous acquired skills and demonstrating many caring and heartfelt actions as well. Look for what they need, and use your heart.

REFERENCES

1. Roberta Trachtman, "Early Childhood Education and Child Care: Issues of At-Risk Children and Families," *Urban Education,* vol. 26 (Apr. 1991): 28.
2. Joy Dryfoos, *Adolescents At-Risk: Prevalence and Prevention* (New York: Oxford Press, 1990), v.
3. Annie Casey Foundation, *Kids Count Data Book, State Profiles of Child Well-Being* (Baltimore: The Foundation, 1994), 5.
4. General Colin Powell. "Opening Remarks." November 25, 1997. Available <www.americaspromise.org/NE4a.htm> Accessed April 28, 1998.
5. Annie Casey Foundation, *Kids Count Data Book, State Profiles of Child Well-Being* (Baltimore: The Foundation, 1996), 5.
6. Annie Casey Foundation, 1996, 5.
7. Council on Adolescent Development, Task Force on Youth Development and Community Programs, *A Matter of Time: Risk and Opportunity in the Nonschool Hours* (New York: The Council, 1992), 33.
8. Council on Adolescent Development, 33.
9. Stan Weisner, *Information Is Empowering: Developing Public Library Services for Youth At-Risk* (Oakland: GRT, 1992), 2.

Chapter 1

Lessons Learned: Making the Case for Library Services for At-Risk Youth

Family income is the clearest determinant of access or lack thereof to community programs for youth, and because life in a poor neighborhood raises adolescents' risks, income is a major factor in determining who is at-risk. More often than not teens who live in poverty, live in unsafe neighborhoods, are unsupervised and are least informed about agencies that provide beneficial services and programs.
—Council on Adolescent Development

Throughout the country there are public libraries in communities where teens live in poverty, surrounded by violence, crime, drug use, and drug trafficking. Public attention and funding for intervention and prevention programs center on four major at-risk behaviors: delinquency, substance abuse, teen pregnancy, and school failure. Although we do not see libraries as lead agencies in addressing any of the major at-risk behaviors, they are emerging as valuable, visible neighborhood-based partners for youth-serving agencies who do specialize in treatment or remediation. In some cases, libraries have initiated action in developing a coalition among youth-serving agencies, and it is nearly always necessary for libraries to initiate the overtures and to create awareness of their potential as partners.

The public library is involved directly in youth development through readers' advisory, special programs, booklists, homework assistance, and career information. These services and activities can serve as positive supports for thousands of youths who may spend a major portion of their nonschool hours engaged in unstructured, unsupervised, unproductive activities. These young people navigate physical danger; cope with boredom, neglect, and abuse; and face uncertain futures. They are the most underserved, and they are the very ones who could benefit from what a library offers. The actual potential of public libraries to help decrease the obstacles that so many of today's at-risk teens face is found in precisely those self-development opportunities they have provided for teens and adults over the past century. Unfortunately, it appears that the importance of using the most powerful strategies to this end has not been fully grasped by teachers, youth workers, or even some librarians themselves.

DEVELOPMENTAL STAGES OF TEENAGERS

For purposes of services and programs, most public libraries define their young adults as 12 to 18. All library staff having contact with this age group should understand as much as possible about the feelings and behaviors that characterize its members. Understandably, each teen's personality is unique, and each has different likes and dislikes; however, extensive research results in a general knowledge base applicable to most teenagers. The American Academy of Child and Adolescent Psychology divides a young person's development into three stages—early, middle, and late. (See Figures 1.1–1.3)

DEVELOPMENTAL TASKS AND NEEDS

There are specific tasks that adolescents need to master if they are to reach responsible adulthood. They need to:

- move toward independence from parents, siblings, and childhood friends while retaining significant and enduring ties.
- develop increasing autonomy in making personal decisions, assuming responsibility for oneself, and regulating one's own behavior.
- establish new friendships.
- move toward greater personal intimacy and adult sexuality.
- face complex intellectual challenges.

In trying to master these tasks, young people have several needs:

- information

Figure 1.1

Early Stage of Adolescent Development
(12–14 years)

Movement towards Independence

- Struggle with sense of identity
- Moodiness
- Improved ability to use speech to express oneself
- More likely to express feelings by action than by words
- Close friendships gain importance
- Less attention shown to parents, with occasional rudeness
- Realization that parents are not perfect; identification of their faults
- Search for new people to love in addition to parents
- Tendency to return to childish behavior, fought off by excessive activity
- Peer group influence interest and clothing styles

Career Interest

- Mostly interested in present and near future
- Greater ability to work

Sexuality

- Girls ahead of boys
- Same-sex friends and group activities
- Shyness, blushing, and modesty
- Show-off qualities
- Greater interest in privacy
- Experimentation with body (masturbation)
- Worries about being normal

Ethics and Self-Direction

- Rule and limit testing
- Occasional experimentation with cigarettes, marijuana, and alcohol
- Capacity for abstract thought

Figure 1.2

Middle Adolescence (15–16 Years)

Movement towards Independence

- Self-involvement, alternating between unrealistically high expectations and poor self-concept
- Complaints that parents interfere with independence
- Extremely concerned with appearance and with one's own body
- Lowered opinion of parents, withdrawal of emotions from them
- Effort to make new friends
- Strong emphasis on the new peer group
- Periods of sadness such as the psychological loss of the parents take place
- Examination of inner experiences, which may include writing a diary

Career Interest

- Intellectual interests gain importance
- Some sexual and aggressive energies directed into creative and career interests

Sexuality

- Concerns about sexual attractiveness
- Frequently changing relationships
- Movement toward heterosexuality with fears of homosexuality
- Tenderness and fears shown towards opposite sex
- Feelings of love and passion

Ethics and Self–Description

- Development of ideals and selection of role models
- More consistent evidence of conscience
- Greater capacity for setting goals
- Interest in moral reasoning

Figure 1.3

Late Adolescence (17–19 years)

Movement towards Independence

- Firmer identity
- Ability to delay gratification
- Ability to express ideas in words
- More developed sense humor
- Stable interests
- Greater emotional stability
- Ability to make independent decisions
- Ability to compromise
- Pride in one's work
- Self-reliance
- Greater concern for others

Career Interest

- More defined work habits
- Higher level of concern for the future
- Thoughts about one's role in life

Sexuality

- Concerned with serious relationships
- Clear sexual identity
- Capacities for tender and sensual love

Ethics and Self–Direction

- Capable of useful insight
- Stress on personal dignity and self-esteem
- Ability to set goals and follow through
- Acceptance of social institutions and cultural traditions
- Self-regulation of self-esteem

- life skills
- critical habits of mind
- dependable relationships
- reliable bases for decision making
- sense of usefulness, need to contribute
- belonging
- autonomy

One major way librarians can play a supportive role in the lives of these teens is to provide creative, diverse programs and services that give young people opportunities to practice developmental tasks. For example, programs that solicit poetry, short stories, and artwork for compilation or display will stimulate and support their need to express inner feelings, experiences, and creative interests. Hot topic forums on sex, drugs, homicide, and curfews led by a qualified local or national professional meet the need young people have to discuss issues and concerns that are most important to them.

While there is no one magic formula for providing effective at-risk youth services, studies are beginning to document long-term best practices, as well as common threads among organizations serving at-risk youth. For example, there are six common traits among people and institutions that run successful programs:[1] (See Figure 1.4)

1. They see genuine potential in the youth they serve; they do not see teenagers as needing to be fixed or controlled, but rather as people largely ignored, wrongly perceived, and badly served by society at large. Still, the most recent brain development research notes that very early deprivation or abuse—referred to as "toxic environments"—can cause damage to later mental and social competence, and some remediation may be in order.

Figure 1.4

Common Needs of At-Risk Youth

- Affection
- Caring
- Nurturing
- Safety
- Structure
- Social support

---

2. They focus on youth. Teenagers receive priority over the organization, the program, or the activity.
3. They believe that their own abilities do make a difference. Far too
many youth workers and policymakers think, "it is too late for
teens." However, successful leaders are convinced that they can and
do make a positive difference in the lives of teens.
4. They feel they are giving back something they owe to a community or society.
5. They view their work as a mission or vocation, not just a job. Their
commitment to young people often stems from what others gave
them during their adolescence.
6. They are authentic. Meshing personal talents, strengths, and getting involved with advocacy on youth's behalf helps to demonstrate
one's authenticity for serving at-risk teens.

Just as there are common developmental needs for teens and common traits of success programs, there are also several factors you will
want to incorporate if you want to develop successful programs for at-
risk youth.

- *Ensure safety.* For youth and adults alike, the fact that no physical
harm will occur is an important part of a successful at-risk program.
- *Listen to youth.* Allow youth to take part in the decision making
and planning for programs of interest and concern to them. Listen
to personal needs.
- *Offer opportunity.* Build the chance for opportunity into the program. At-risk youth want the chance to break out of the boundaries imposed by their surroundings. They long to imagine and
experience the unimagined or unimaginable.
- *Provide real responsibilities, real work.* Young people need to have
a sense of real responsibilities and real work. Significant programs
result in developing a sense of being valuable to the broader society, and at the same time such programs have clear significance to
the local community.
- *Establish clear rules and discipline.* "Contrary to many adults' assumptions, at-risk youth are especially uncomfortable in anything-
goes environments,"[2] and they often test an adult's level of caring
and commitment. At the same time, they tend not to stay in settings where rules are too rigid or unfair or where discipline seems
erratic or harsh
- *Focus on the future.* Help youth to develop a sense of how valu-

able education is. "Education is not treated as a virtue in and of itself but as a means to achieving a positive future." At-risk youth "need tools for their own future, not just skills, but the pride and discipline to work hard to achieve goals."[3]

- *Foster resiliency.* Resiliency is a significant trait allowing many at-risk youth to cope and succeed despite the odds. Studies show that in order to achieve resilience young people often need but one caring and supportive adult to believe in them and to guide them into successful adulthood.[4] Educational and social support institutions—such as schools and libraries—are natural environments in which empathic adults may be found who will help nurture the resilience of the at-risk individual. According to Emmy Werner of the University of California, resilient youth who are able to overcome family and other deficits have four common characteristics:[5]

1. An active, vigorous approach to solving life's problems.
2. Tendencies to perceive their experiences constructively even if they involve pain or suffering.
3. The ability, from infancy on, to gain other people's positive attention.
4. A strong ability to maintain a positive vision of a meaningful life.

CARING AND THE WELCOMING ENVIRONMENT

By the time many youth, especially minority teens, have reached adolescence, they have experienced the slings and arrows of subtle and overt discriminations. They recognize the slights and destructive attitudes of a great number of service providers. They have learned to avoid places where they think and feel no one cares for them or will welcome their presence. Their lives have been

> . . . affected by the erosion of family and educational supports, especially among the poor and socially isolated, leaving them lonely and with a feeling of having no control over their destiny. What kind of social support do adolescents need? Three ingredients are needed: aid, affirmation, and affect. Aid refers to practical services and material benefits needed for development. Affirmation refers to feedback that raises self-esteem and strengthens identity. Affect refers to the provision of affection, caring, and nurturance.[6]

In other words, adolescents need practical assistance, positive feedback, affection, care, and nurturing.

Research shows that often a major contributing factor to the success or failure of similar programs offered in different locations is the environment. Is it welcoming? Is it caring? Caring includes helping, explaining, encouraging, guiding, and listening. Being welcoming means being sensitive, friendly (but never invasive), interested, tolerant, receptive, responsive, and respectful. Libraries with appropriate collections, services, and programs can provide crucial emotional, cognitive, and social support for at-risk youth. They can also offer programs that teach relevant and practical life skills. Ideally, a youth-centered library is accessible, safe, and offers challenging opportunities that appeal to the diverse interests of youth.

PREPARING TO SERVE

Providing services to at-risk teens is a time-consuming and often a daunting task. It is important to anticipate and develop strategies that minimize or overcome possible obstacles or challenges. First, it is important to seek commitment and support from essential stakeholders for the concept of serving at-risk teenagers. The stakeholders would be the library director, library board members, friends of the library, school personnel, and members of various community organizations.

Encourage your supporters to voice any concerns and issues they may have during this time, and solicit their recommendations for resolving their concerns. For example, someone might fear that your traditional programming might be short-changed or worry about funding and staffing. Encourage that person and others to help you determine if there can be an equitable balance between "traditional" and "nontraditional" services, and if so, what that balance would be. There are no pat answers to questions like this, but with thoughtful negotiation and willingness to compromise it is possible to strike a reasonable medium for all stakeholders.

It is also useful to become familiar with various social work applications regarding at-risk youth. You will need to have contacts with community groups, psychologists, youth organizations, and advocacy groups. If this is not possible, try to consult with a local professional social worker or professional youth worker. He or she may serve as a technical advisor and serve as a link to teenagers in your area and other youth-serving organizations.

The bottom line is, you are most likely to be successful if participating staff members sincerely like teens, are able to relate to young people in an outreach setting, and can demonstrate genuine caring and enthusiasm.

TRAINING

Among the major obstacles to effective service to at-risk teens are lack of skills and training. Without the requisite skills, even those who sincerely wish to provide special services will be unable to. Adequate training was a major contributing factor to the success of the Bay Area Library and Information Service (BALIS) Youth-At-Risk project. For example, the staff at the Berkeley Public Library conducted an all-staff development workshop to heighten awareness of teen needs and share knowledge related to teens in general. The staff who will encounter teens as well as the staff who make policy and funding decisions should be sensitive to the plight of at-risk teens. They need to understand a few critical facts, such as teen needs, general facts about teens, their role in helping, and the library's proposed plans for service and programs. An all-staff development workshop, featuring a knowledgeable motivational speaker, is an ideal way to begin the training process. Also, be certain to determine the staff's mastery of those "nuts and bolts" skills required for implementing this service. In addition to staff who can work directly with youth on a day-to-day basis, it is also helpful to have staff who can write press releases, develop programs, develop flyers, and are able to form and work with teen advisory groups. You will also want staff to have some counseling skills, if possible, and planning skills, such as the ability to conduct a needs assessment. The range of desirable skills is listed in Figure 1.6. The BALIS Youth-At-Risk project and the successful application of these skills are covered in the remaining chapters.

Figure 1.5

Sample Workshop

TRAINING SESSION FLYERS

BAY AREA YOUTH

"At-Risk" of What? and Why?

A SPECIAL TRAINING SESSION FOR BAY AREA YOUTH ADULT
LIBRARIANS/AND OTHER INTERESTED LIBRARY STAFF

Hosted by the BALIS-Sponsored Bay Area Youth-at-Risk Project

PROGRAM

"Models of Risk-Taking Behavior among Adolescents"

- Jenny Broering, M.D., C.P.N.P.
- Associate Clinical Professor
- Division of Adolescent Medicine, UCSF

PLUS!

"Communicating with Adolescents—"
A Skills Workshop

Alice Wilkins, LCSW
Berkeley Psychotherapist and Trainer

Thursday, March 28, 1991
8:30 A.M. – 12:30 P.M.

The program will be held a West Auditorium,
Oakland Public Library
Located at 125 and 14th Street. Refreshments will be served at 8:30
A.M. and the workshops will begin
promptly at 9:00 A.M.

Figure 1.6
Knowledge, Skills, and Training Checklist

- Counseling techniques
- Knowledge of basic youth development principles
- How to collaborate with other agencies
- How to mobilize adults and youth to assess and address ways to effectively serve this group
- Knowledge of different cultures and ethnic values
- Ability to work with youth and families from diverse cultures
- Strategies for gaining outside funding
- Knowledge of programs that are effective and innovative in serving at-risk youth
- How to recruit volunteers who are skilled at working with at-risk youth
- How to conduct and analyze a needs assessment

REFERENCES

1. Mibrey W. McLaughlin, Merita Irgy, and Juliet Langman, *Urban Sanctuaries: Neighborhood Organizations in the Lives and Futures of Inner-City Youth* (San Francisco: Josey-Bass, 1994), 96-103.
2. McLaughlin, et al., 109.
3. McLaughlin et al., 110.
4. McLaughlin et al., 110.
5. McLaughlin et al., 110.
6. Joy Dryfoos, "School-Based Social and Health Services for At-Risk Students," *Urban Education,* 26 (April 1991): 121.

Chapter 2

Public Library Service for Youth-at-Risk: The San Francisco Bay Area Models

The role of the public library in serving-at risk youth will never be the same again. The Bay Area Youth-At-Risk Project (YAR) has put teen-agers firmly on the agenda of public libraries, and more importantly, has enabled libraries to actively participate in the network of front-line, youth services agencies active in developing preventive services to teens in the 1990s.

—Stan Weisner

BACKGROUND: THE BAY AREA PROJECT

Stan Weisner, project director of the "Youth-At-Risk Bay Area Project," made this optimistic observation about the changed role of the library on September 30, 1991, during a press conference at the Oakland Public Library.[1] In 1988, the California Library Services Board had allocated priority funding for services to youth at risk. With that incentive, in 1990 BALIS initiated plans to provide special library services to young people at risk. In 1990 the state received the monies, a Library Services and Construction Act (LSCA) award, to support the project. So it was with great anticipation that the Bay Area Library and Information System (BALIS) unveiled plans to provide special library services to young people at risk. At that time, a quarter of a million teens, aged 12 to 18, lived in the counties of Alameda, Contra Costa, and San Francisco. The project targeted adolescents "whose potential of becoming healthy and productive adults is reduced because they are at high risk of encountering serious problems at home, in school, or in their communities."[2]

Youth between 12 and 18 who might perhaps engage or had already engaged in "risk-taking behaviors" (i.e., substance abuse, delinquency, teen pregnancy, school failure) were included in the project. However, the project targeted primarily those youths aged 12 to 18 who were believed to be at high or moderately high levels of risk. There were nine participating libraries: Alameda City, Alameda County, Berkeley Public, Contra Costa County, Hayward Public, Oakland Public, Livermore Public, Richmond Public, and San Francisco Public. (see Figure 2.1)

THE PROCESS

Plans for this much needed service began in 1990 when the state received the LSCA monies. Participants involved in the initial planning phase included staff from each of the participating libraries, representatives from many community organizations, at-risk youth, project staff, and consultants. The planning process in general followed the steps and terms used in *Planning and Role Setting for Public Libraries.*[3] Three crucial components—staff training, coalition building, and determining youth needs guided the planning outcomes. The specialized training built the staff's confidence in serving teens from diverse, often unfamiliar, backgrounds. Further, the training created an opportunity for staff to learn about teen issues and to gain knowledge of techniques used to enhance services that would get the attention of at-risk youth. In order to craft a meaningful role for the libraries, it was understood that it was essential to involve at-risk teens and a variety of their other service providers. They all gave invaluable insight, support, and recommendations.

Each of the libraries conducted a needs assessment with hundreds of Bay Area teenagers and their other service providers. The needs assessments revealed that libraries could play a supportive partnership role for these neighborhood-based, youth-serving agencies that addressed issues such as substance abuse, gang violence, and teen pregnancy. The assessments allowed for the identification of the "individual needs of youth from the very basic (food, clothing, and shelter) to higher level needs including education, recreation, and nurturing."[4] Equipped with comprehensive community needs assessments, high levels of community involvement, and extensive staff training, each participating library developed strategies to expand and improve services for this audience.

	Figure 2.1	
	BALIS Youth-At-Risk Project Needs and Pilot Projects	
Library	**Priority Need**	**Select Pilot Project**
Alameda County (San Lorenzo Branch)	Multicultural exchange; job training	Teen forums on key issues; distribution of resource guide; "Stump the Librarian" contest
Alameda Free	Awareness of youth-related services/programs; improved school performance	Tutoring clearinghouse; teen room improvement
Berkeley	Teen employment and youth involvement in library programming	Youth Outreach Corps and media outreach (PSA)
Contra Costa County (San Pablo Branch)	Awareness of services; coordination with youth-serving agencies	Video outreach project to schools and youth-serving agencies; hip-pocket guide distributed to services
Hayward	Access to neighborhood-based services and information on resources; school-dropout prevention	Youth forums and school outreach; hip-pocket resource guide; teen issues pamphlet and resource file
Livermore	Improved school performance; teen employment opportunities	Develop teen area; teen information booklet "Under 18 and Unhappy at Home?"
Oakland (M.L. King Branch)	Improved coordination with agencies/schools; school-dropout prevention	Tutoring outreach in public housing
Richmond	School drop-out prevention; coordination with youth-serving agencies	Tutoring program support to youth-serving agencies; hip-pocket resource guide
San Francisco	Access to information by/for African American and immigrant youth	Youth fee amnesty; develop out-stationed library services in public housing, Youth Guidance Center, etc.; cooperative projects with youth-serving organizations

THE NINE PROJECTS

During the fall of 1991, the libraries implemented a varied range of programs specifically designed to expand and improve library services to at-risk youth. Overall, the libraries implemented a rich variety of demonstration projects ranging from creating jobs, designing and disseminating resource guides, and providing tutoring to building special teen collections. The staff at the participating libraries embraced the opportunity to address the needs and concerns of young people in communities throughout the San Francisco Bay Area.

Alameda Free Library

Doing well in school emerged as the major concern among the city of Alameda's 5,000 teens. The needs assessment revealed a lack of awareness of library resources or available services for youth from other providers. The library developed an awareness campaign by printing and distributing material specifically targeted for teens. Middle and high school youth received 5,000 informative book covers. The library distributed several thousand hip-pocket guides to youth services. The library also created a larger young adult space. Plans to serve as a clearinghouse for tutors were not implemented because the number of students desiring to use the service exceeded the number of tutors. However, the staff felt they succeeded in their effort to raise awareness of the library as a resource for teens.

Berkeley Public Library

As in other areas, the library discovered that a large majority of Berkeley's 7,000 teens knew very little about the resources offered by the library. However, in Berkeley, African-American and Hispanic youth identified employment as the most significant unmet need. Berkeley Public responded with the Youth Outreach Corps, which included employing three teens to assist the library staff in reaching out to other young people. Several creative public service announcements were developed and aired in the local media and helped to raise awareness of library and community services among teens. The central library held a youth rap and poetry program. It enhanced its young adult collection by purchasing videos that dealt with health and mental health. The library also conducted a successful all-staff workshop on awareness of the problems, attitudes, and needs of at-risk youth.

Contra Costa County Library

The Contra Costa County Library discovered many of its 63,000 teens were poorly served; they had no information on youth services, there was no coordination among the area's other youth-serving agencies, and the library had no outreach program to these agencies. In response to the assessment, the library produced and distributed a hip-pocket teen resource guide, referring youth to agencies that could provide direct assistance with crisis issues. The library developed a collection of video and print "discussion starter" materials and publicized their use for organizations and persons who served young people, especially in the San Pablo area.

Along with the neighboring Richmond Public Library, the San Pablo Branch worked to improve outreach and bring youth-serving agencies together. Together they cohosted quarterly meetings among community-based organizations serving at-risk youth. Participation in the meeting increased during the grant period from 8 to 60 organizations. With programs on homework help, library-access skills and multicultural awareness, the San Pablo Library also reached out to a junior high school Asian youth group.

Hayward Public Library

School-dropout prevention programs and increased access to supportive neighborhood-based services were major needs among Hayward's 9,000 young people. The library responded by providing speakers in neighborhood settings on useful topics, including finding and holding a job and staying free of drugs. The library developed a resource file of pamphlets on important topics for distribution to teens and distributed a hip-pocket resource guide created by the Southern Alameda County Network of Youth Services. The library also held a well-received program titled "Let's Talk about Sex."

Livermore Public Library

The need to be successful in school was high on Livermore's 5,000 teens' list. Younger teens found peer relationships challenging and older ones expressed concern about obtaining future employment. Numerous young people were unaware of library services, and those youth familiar with the library disapproved of the requirement that persons under 18 needed a parent's signature to receive a library card.

Livermore Public Library collaborated with other agencies to produce and distribute widely a booklet titled "Under 18 and Unhappy at Home?" This guide assisted teens with contact information for help with problems. The library changed its registration policy to allow young people 16 and older with identification to receive a card. There was an increase in programs about finding jobs and developing interviewing skills, and they held workshops on vocational opportunities after high school. The library hired additional young people as library aides and pages. They also purchased more nonfiction for young adults, printed and distributed 4,000 bookmarks, and began production of a video about online computer use.

Oakland Public Library

The top problems facing Oakland's 31,000 teenagers were dropping out of school and below-grade literacy levels. The library's Martin Luther King Jr. Branch in East Oakland responded by instituting an after school tutoring/homework center. The library recruited tutors beyond those who worked in youth agency tutorial programs.

Even though the program was designed to serve 12- to 15-year-olds, about 130 young people between the ages of 10 and 15 signed up for the program. Saturday morning proved to be the best time for the tutoring service. Over 200 hundred people attended the informative and entertaining program "The Politics of Rap" hosted by a local disc jockey.

Richmond Public Library

Richmond's 7,700 young people needed support to overcome low literacy skills and a high dropout rate. The library worked closely with two community-based organizations and offered its new Tutoring Library Connection service. The service offered materials and speakers to support the community-based organizations' tutorial programs.

Richmond Public Library also distributed a hip-pocket resource guide to youth services published in partnership with the Contra Costa County Library. As mentioned earlier, they also cohosted quarterly meetings of community-based organizations with Contra Costa County Library. To combat literacy problems and a high dropout rate they developed a tutor referral list and promoted their tutoring outreach at a local career fair.

San Francisco Public Library

The needs assessment on behalf of San Francisco's 45,000 teens showed that middle school youth from African-American, Latino, and limited-English-speaking groups had problems in accessing information to help with poverty, education, health, discrimination, and newcomer adjustment. To address these issues, the Bayview-Anna E. Waden Branch of the San Francisco Public Library created a Teen Corner with a larger collection. To develop a model for offsite services and deposit collections their outreach efforts focused on establishing library services at the Youth Guidance Center (Juvenile Hall). Multiethnic, multilingual residents received fiction and nonfiction books and popular magazines on a weekly basis.

LIBRARY MODELS

As a result of a thorough analysis of the BALIS project, six categories of services emerged as models useful to libraries in providing services to at-risk teens.

1. Providing Information About Services

Youth need basic information about services in their community. The library serves as the intermediary between youth and other community resources. Directories may range from a creative hip pocket guide to a very simple listing in bookmark form. Sharing this type of information in useful portable formats also benefits the library through additional publicity and encourages greater use.

2. Young Adult Collection and Facility Development

This is a relative easy model to implement if the funds are available. It involves customizing the collection to reflect the needs of this target audience with books, periodicals, videos, tapes, and compact discs; upgrading signage; and purchasing new shelving and furniture.

3. Programs For Youth

This innovative model enables the library to raise its visibility as a resource, collaborate with others, and focus on youth culture. Special programs for at-risk teens may relate indirectly or directly to the library. These can include outreach efforts like talent night or various contests— art, poetry, short story writing, photography, and dance. Also, forums on teen issues such as drugs, violence, music, and obtaining jobs, cosponsored with other youth-serving agencies, can become annual events involving a wider section of the community. It is important to remember that young people may have hidden interests, private preserves not common to the perception of the "youth culture," to which the library's resources may relate.

4. Tutoring Programs

Libraries help to enhance the academic skills of teens through formal and informal homework assistance, organizing tutorial programs, and serving as a clearinghouse between community tutoring resources and interested students. Tutoring programs are often difficult to implement because of the logistics of scheduling volunteers and students. However, finding a committed adult volunteer to serve as the coordinator of this meaningful service minimizes a tremendous range of problems.

5. Community Outreach

Taking library resources outside of the physical building provides the librarian with the opportunity to be seen in a different setting and reach a wider audience. Participating in community- or other youth-serving agency-sponsored events like fairs, block parties, and career days, also affirms the library's role as an integral part of the community.

6. Integrating Youth into the Library

Selecting youth as employees or volunteers addresses teen needs for jobs and job skills. Librarians may also get to know more about other young people in the community and determine how they can best address some of their needs and interests.

REFERENCES

1. Stan Weisner, *Information Is Empowering: Developing Public Library Services for Youth At-Risk* (Oakland: GRT, 1992), 164.
2. David Hamburg, *Today's Children: Creating a Future for a Generation in Crisis* (New York: Random House, 1992), 104.
3. Hamburg, 254.
4. Weisner, viii.

Chapter 3

Strategies for Gaining Support

The trends are irrefutable: American's youth are becoming more and more diverse in cultural, ethnic and socioeconomic backgrounds. . . . The nation faces growing concerns about rising numbers of other youth who are vulnerable and trapped in high-risk situations.

—Eugene Roehlkepartain

In recognition of these facts, numerous youth-serving organizations are making serious attempts to reach out and serve those presently beyond the reach of their programs and services. Turning the tide and improving the life options of these teens require the collaborative efforts of not only schools but of other local government agencies such as libraries, community-based organizations, and other youth-serving agencies. In many cases organizations need to make significant changes to become more effective and efficient in their delivery of services to this group. For libraries located in high-risk communities, an aggressive proactive attitude accompanied by the question, "How can we better serve?" will minimize staff stress and ultimately result in improved services to teens. It is important to realize that many of these young people know nothing of most library services and the resources that exist or even that such services or resources could be of any possible interest or use to them.

The completion of an external needs assessment of at-risk teens in the library service district is an essential beginning for creating programs and services. It is also necessary to conduct a realistic and thorough internal assessment of all library resources needed to serve this audience. This includes staff skills, collection size and relevance, types of programs, level of funding, library size, hours of service, and necessary staff training. Public school systems serving at-risk teens are often criticized and held accountable for poorly educating them and for below average retention rates. Many public libraries in those same service areas face similar issues, in addition to lack of use by at-risk teens, insufficient specialized staff, and limited funding. Yet, just as the general public, politicians, and funding sources hold public school administrators and teachers accountable for their performances in educating at-risk youth, I for one will welcome the day when library administrators and librarians are held far more accountable for their performances in serving this segment of our population. In the near future, it should no longer be acceptable to place the onus entirely on at-risk youth for failure to use the library. The public library at the very least can develop collections and implement relevant services and programs for this group.

The library staff, community members, and other youth serving agencies need to arrive at a consensus regarding services, programs, and strategies if the venture is to be a success. Therefore, they all should play an active role in both the needs assessment process and the final planning initiatives. A news story or public plea challenging professionals to serve as tutors for low-income youth in a public library, may provide the spark for community organizations to approach the library or vice versa to discuss special services for at-risk youth. A successful venture in this area could also provide the impetus for an initial dialogue with library administrators and staff to examine the effectiveness of current services for this group. A useful resource to use in the examination of the effectiveness of your services, is *Planning for Results: A Public Library Transformation Process* (1998).[1] This book is a major revision *Planning and Role Setting for Public Libraries* (1987)[2] used by the BALIS Youth-At-Risk Project.

ADMINISTRATIVE SUPPORT

Ideally, the library director sets the tone and creates the environment in which the desire to serve at-risk youth will flourish. The director's determined commitment to this complex but essential undertaking is absolutely necessary. Indeed, in the BALIS projects, the active involvement

> "In my twenty-four years of work with at-risk youth, I have never collaborated with the public library." (Kirby Burgess, director of Family and Youth Service, Clark County, Las Vegas, Nevada).

of the library directors was viewed as essential to getting started and sustaining the project. The librarian activist initiator may need to provide the director with complete information about at-risk teens. Collect local and national data regarding their plight and the cost to individuals and the society at large of low literacy and delinquency. Presenting a possible plan of action on the part of the library is a good starting point. An excellent statistical and narrative starting point is to review the latest *Kids Count Data Book: State Profiles of Child Well-Being.*[3] *Kids Count* is published annually by the Annie E. Casey Foundation, a national organization dedicated exclusively to serving at-risk youth. It is a state-by-state initiative that tracks the status of young people in the U.S. and provides policy makers and service providers with benchmarks of child well-being. *Kids Count* uses the best available data to measure the educational, social, economic, and physical well-being of young people. Additionally, "Fedstats: One Stop Shopping for Federal Statistics" is a great website to access for a variety of federal government statistics <http://www.fedstats.gov/>.

STAFF SUPPORT

If the library director gives the green light to proceed with the development of a service or program for at-risk teens, one must rally staff support, not only in the youth department, but also throughout the library. A useful strategy to begin to gain support of other library staff is to hold an in-service training day that focuses on young adults. The Berkeley Public Library did quite successfully (see Chapter Five). It may also prove beneficial to prepare a fact sheet for staff that would include basic local statistics about at-risk youth, their families/caregivers, and their communities (see Figure 3.1). One could present a low-cost, interesting project in which the staff enjoys "collaborating" in the development and implementation phases like "Trading Places" or "Talent Galore" (see Chapter Seven). Be sure to document and write up the activity for the staff newsletter or local community paper, and do take advantage of the public opportunity to thank all who assisted with the program. Figure 3.2 is an article from a staff newsletter that describes "Trading Places," a program in which six young people traded places with library staff for a day.

There are several approaches the library can take to establish contact with community organizations. One is to compile a list of community youth-serving organizations. This will include both voluntary membership organizations; private and publicly-supported agencies; and local

---

Figure 3.1

Caroline Library Community Profile

805 FAMILES LIVE IN THE COMMUNITY—
85% ON PUBLIC ASSISTANCE

There are a total of 2,362 residents:

1,148 are adults

1,214 are minors

The average family size is 3.13

44% of the adults did not complete high school

There are 546 children over six years old

There are 202 infants/toddlers

There are 204 preschoolers

There are 536 teens between the ages of 12 and 19

---

government units, such as police departments and parks and recreation departments. Often information about local community-based organizations can be found in the mayor's office of children and youth, and in many cases the library will have pamphlets and directories of community organizations.

It will make the collaboration process more manageable if at first you establish contact with one or two major youth service providers who can, in turn, assist with advice and gaining the support of other community groups. Initial contact can be accomplished through a telephone call, followed up with a written letter or memo, and then a personal visit. In the first discussion you should not only obtain detailed information regarding the agency or organization's ongoing programs and goals, but also share the library's ideas for serving at-risk teens and helping the partner agency support and implement its own objectives. Encourage feedback and suggestions and solicit recommendations as to who else may be of assistance in the common endeavor. Remember, many experienced youth providers have techniques, expertise, and support systems that will serve the intentions of the library well. You may also wish to approach a particular youth-serving agency and offer support by providing meeting room space, booklists, and special materials to support their programs and assisting in communicating their objectives. Gradually a list of common goals and objectives will evolve in part supplanting "yours" and "mine" with "ours."

Figure 3.2

Trading Places

"Y'all get to sit a lot on this job." "All you have to do is answer the phone and show people where the books are." "If I were in charge, I would . . . ." These comments among several from young adults, reflecting their confused and distorted perceptions of what is involved in library work, led to "Trading Places," a one-day program conceived by the staff of the Hollins-Payson Branch. The objective was to increase communication and understanding by providing a group of young adults with the opportunity to experience the "upstairs/downstairs" activities of a public library.

The response from the young people to the idea of trading places with the library staff was not only favorable, but enthusiastic. The six available positions—Branch Librarian, Adult Services Librarian, Children's Librarian, Desk Supervisor, Desk Assistant, and Security Guard—were filled within an hour of the announcement. Orientation for each young adult consisted of an appointment with the staff member whose job he/she had and the time was spent explaining job descriptions and attendant duties. Gradually, the branch staff began to notice that the excitement about the program had spread beyond the selected participants to other young adults who used the branch. Many questions about how the program worked, how each person was chosen, and what the jobs entailed, in addition to visible signs of disappointment from those who were not chosen for the "jobs," were positive indicators of genuine interest.

On the morning of the big day, the eager "Trading Places staff" arrived at the branch early, anxious to begin. The morning was spent at the Central Library. Greeted by the gracious Personnel Office staff, the young adults received their identification badges, filled out application forms, and were given a thorough first-day-at-work orientation by Daphne Hurd. A whirlwind tour of the Central Library followed. A festive luncheon at the Chinese Gourmet Restaurant, courtesy of Deborah Taylor, Young Adult Services Specialist, was one of the high points of the day. Comments after lunch included: "The food was good"; "We're ready to work"; and "Take more pictures."

Back at the branch for the afternoon, the young people performed a variety of tasks, including patron assistance, registration, scheduling, book revision, and charging out books. When we gathered at the end of the day for a final photograph of the library staff with the Trading Places staff, we sensed that something very special had occurred amongst all those involved in the program. They left proud; we left pleased.

JoAnn G. Mondowney
Hollins-Payson Branch

NETWORKING

Networking involves building relationships with various community members and groups in order to communicate, solve problems related to similar issues and concerns, and to gain invaluable support. The following pointers will help you create an effective network of people.

- Learn about all teens for they will encompass and have many of the attributes of the target population.
- Get to know community workers, especially those who work on a daily basis with target teens and their families.
- Find a seasoned community worker who is willing to be a mentor.
- Make the acquaintance of principals and teachers. Be prepared for the reality that many of them may not understand the potential of the role of the library.
- Attend meetings and other programs involving at-risk youth.
- Attend workshops and social events with staff from other youth-serving agencies.

Collaboration

Opportunities abound for collaboration with other organizations serving at-risk teens. The library might want to support a group seeking special funding for a program by providing in-kind services, such as space and library materials. Alternatively, it may choose to serve as a clearinghouse for providing information about community organizations. Many programs in the BALIS project were completed as a result of collaborative efforts with other organizations. The appendix has a list of support and partnership opportunities with organizations that serve at-risk children and youth.

YOUTH ADVISORY GROUPS

Research shows that successful at-risk programs seek input from young people during the initial planning and implementation stages. It is important for librarians responsible for designing programs and services to encourage constructive dialogue between the library staff and the youth they are going to serve. The best way to solicit input from youth and others who serve them is to form a youth advisory group. An advisory group made up of teens and adults will yield the best of both possible worlds. With guidance, teens will express their needs and wants, and they will come up with ways the library can be of help to them. Establishing an advisory group also allows for:

- greater community consensus and responsiveness in planning;
- implementating at-risk programs and services;
- increased visibility for the library;
- new opportunities to foster collaborative activities among youth-service groups, but also with private businesses;
- a means to improve community relations; and
- a unified voice for teen advocacy.

Working with young people and several youth-serving organizations to gain broad representation and input for the project or service can be complex and quite a challenge. Frequently it is filled with logistical nightmares and obstacles. Often, people have little experience in working with initiatives that cross racial, class, and cultural lines. It is necessary to develop an appreciation of and understanding for the diversity of language, variety of styles, difference in beliefs, types of lifestyles, and numerous interests when working with people from various community organizations.

Committee Development

Once the library decides to create a youth advisory group, either one composed of teens and interested adults or an adult group and a teen group, the following steps are necessary to provide focus and direction for the groups:

- Draft the committee charge (purpose and estimated life of the committee).
- Determine essential players.
- Determine best meeting times and location.
- Develop mailing list.
- Develop productive agendas.
- Be clear about why the committee exists.
- Articulate the committee's mandate in terms of limitations and opportunities.
- Seek diverse membership that reflects the community (e.g., gender, ethnicity, age, etc.)

Figure 3.3

Sample Meeting Agenda

YOUTH AT-RISK STEERING COMMITTEE MEETING AGENDA

4:00-4:15   Welcome and Introductions

4:15-4:30   Review of Methods Used to Collect Needs
              Assessment data
              Interviews
              Focus groups
              Mailed questionnaires

4:30-4:45   Presentation of Draft Report
              Basic demographics
              Major identified needs
              Young adult services recommendations

4:45-4:55   Discussion
              Review and critique report
              Consensus on priorities
              What is feasible?
              Additional information needed

5:45-6:00   Future Role of YAR Steering Committee
              Ongoing advisory role
              Review pilot project in second year
              Timeline for remainder of needs assessment

- Try to include someone in the adult youth advisory group who has foundation or corporate giving contacts. If you think additional funding might be required for a new service or project.

Meeting Logistics

The techniques listed below will help to run meetings that are productive and not unduly time consuming:

- Keep the committee's needs and availability in mind.
- Consider holding meetings away from the library if it is more convenient for the majority of the group.

- Plan meeting and notify participants of dates three to four weeks in advance.
- Send out an advance agenda (see Figure 3.3 a sample meeting agenda).
- Telephone the members the day before to confirm the meeting.

How to Run a Meeting

It is essential to determine before the meeting what needs to be accomplished and to have in mind some strategies for producing the desired outcomes. This will enable you to focus, develop an effective agenda, and remain on task during the meeting.

- Welcome attendees.
- Point out restrooms.
- Pass around attendance sheet (ask for name, affiliation, address, telephone, fax, and e-mail).
- Serve light refreshments.
- Ask each attendee to fill out and wear a nametag.
- Ask for introductions from everyone.

At the first meeting you could pair off the participants and have them briefly interview each other—name, association, expectations, special talent or area of expertise, and interests or concerns as they relate to at-risk teens. Then ask each pair to introduce each other to the group.

- If necessary, select a facilitator in advance to encourage participation and to keep the meeting focused and on schedule.
- Use a flip chart and/or tape recorder to document major issues, summarize actions, and record follow-up tasks.
- Record notes or minutes from the meeting. Edit the information and send highlights and actions to the participants.
- Send roster of attendees with the meeting notes or minutes.

STORIES AND STATISTICS

Statistical data and personal stories help create a vivid picture of who is at risk where, both nationally and locally. For example, a report about at-risk teens who took advantage of the library's homework tutorial pilot project is greatly enhanced by including their selected personal comments and their stories about the experience. These comments help the library gain additional support to continue or expand a service. In addition, always solicit and document comments from staff.

In 1994, the *Kids Count Data Book* focused entirely on the well-being of at-risk children and youth in the United States. Statistical data in the 1994 *Kids Count* edition included information about education, teen pregnancy, teen violence, and the percentage of teens graduating from high school on time in all states. To complement this extensive statistical document, the Casey Foundation sponsored the publication *Kids' Voices Count.*[4] The book profiled young people at risk throughout the country. Teens shared poignant stories with peer interviewers. In addition, the teen interviewers recorded their own thoughtful and astute observations concerning the young people they interviewed. Together, the two complementary pieces made a powerful statement about the plight of at-risk youth. This is a perfect example of how to wed stories and statistics and earn needed support for a special service.

The BALIS project created videos to help document and tell a more effective story. Customized, well-done videos are quite effective in making the case for helping teens. The Bureau for At-Risk Youth publishes *At-Risk Resources*, where you will find a variety of useful videos to help you create your stories. These videos are also good to use at in-service training meetings and to show at meetings of your youth advisory groups. For example, *Survivor's Pride*, a 60-minute video about building resilience in youth at-risk is very good. Drs. Steven and Sybil Wolin, experts in the field of resiliency, show ways to use resiliency-oriented prevention and intervention techniques. Another good choice is *Job Search Skills for At-Risk Students*, a three-part video series that covers search skills, resume tips, and interview techniques in a way that provides guidance for at-risk teens and those who want to help. For information on how to obtain these videos, contact the Bureau for At-Risk Youth at 1-800-999-6884.

REFERENCES

1. Ethel E. Himmel and William James Wilson, *Planning for Results: A Public Library Transformation Process* (Chicago: American Library Association, 1998).
2. Charles R. McClure et al., *Planning and Role Setting for Public Libraries: A Manual of Options and Procedures* (Chicago: American Library Association, 1987).
3. Annie Casey Foundation, *Kids Count Data Book, State Profiles of Child Well-Being* (Baltimore: The Foundation, Annual).
4. Jessica Beels, *Kids' Voices Count: Illuminating the Statistics.* (Washington: Children's Express, 1994).

Chapter 4

Conducting a Youth
Needs Assessment

Never do what you would not have known.
—Chinese Proverb

*We did a number of focus groups with teens. Many things we
knew already, which validated a lot of things we thought about the
community. And we also found out some things we didn't know.*
—Regina Minudri

The youth needs assessment process affords the library staff the chance
to interact with and involve teens, social workers, parents, and other
youth-serving organizations. This comprehensive process generates detailed information about at-risk youth ranging from demographics, family income, and education levels to health and mortality rates. An accurate
analysis aids in developing a solid rationale for making decisions about
programs and services and tends to enhance the degree of commitment
from participants in the process. If you have limited time, no experience,
and want an objective point of view, hire a consultant to conduct the
assessment.

THE ASSESSMENT PROCESS

Completing the following activities before you start will make the assessment process easier.

Figure 4.1

Youth Needs Assessment Definition

Youth needs assessment: a study that identifies the individual needs of youth—from the very basic needs of food, clothing, and shelter to higher level needs including education, recreation, and nurturing. The study allows you to determine the degree to which the needs are being met.

---

1. Define the target group (e.g., at-risk youth ages 12-18 in a specific area).
2. Place the community in perspective, become familiar with key demographic and economic information; with youth serving organizations, with at-risk youth activities, and with issues and concerns that affect their lives.
3. Develop a list of potential participants who can assist with the process.
4. Develop a work plan to define the scope of what needs to be accomplished and to provide an approximate timeline for completion of the assessment process.

The process involves creation of an appropriate research instrument to supply useful information, questionnaires, interviews, focus groups, and data analysis. While your input is required, the assistance of an experienced consultant is likely to yield more valid results and builds staff confidence in their ability to present findings to various funding sources and future supporters. Check with nearby colleges or local research firms for pro bono (free of charge) or discount fees. If there are fees, then the library and consultant should sign a written contract (see Figure 4.2) that describes the work and the timetable for its completion.

Figure 4.2

Sample Consultant's Contract

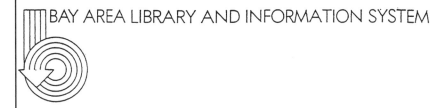

BAY AREA LIBRARY AND INFORMATION SYSTEM

STANDARD AGREEMENT

THIS AGREEMENT, made and entered into this _____ day of _____, 19 ___, by and between the Bay Area Library Information System, State of California, hereinafter called the System, and _____ hereinafter called the Contractor.

WITNESSETH: That the Contractor for and in consideration of the covenants, conditions, agreements, and stipulations of the System hereinafter expressed, does hereby agree to furnish to the System services and materials, as follows, and/or as described on exhibits attached to and incorporated herein.

(Set forth: 1) Service to be rendered by Contract; 2) Program receiving service 3) Contractor's qualifications; 4) Additional provisions incorporated.)

Design and implement study of youth at risk in San Francisco which will include interviews (10-15 face-to-face; 30-40 telephone) with key informants, and 3-4 focus groups.

Complete written needs assessment and draft recommendations on Young Adult library services in 30-40 page report that includes findings from interviews and focus groups and incorporates data from provider survey and demographic data.

Present draft report to San Francisco Youth-At-Risk team and prepare final report by July 31, 1991.

FIGURE 4.2 — _Continued_

CONTRACT PERIOD will be from _____

through _____.

COMPENSATION: System agrees to pay Contractor for services
performed hereunder at the rate of $_____ per _____
and/or in accordance with the following payment schedule:

The total amount paid by System to Contractor under this agreement shall not exceed the sum of $_____.

ADDITIONAL PROVISIONS set forth on the reverse hereof constitute a part of this agreement.

IN WITNESS WHEREOF, the parties hereto have executed this
agreement as of the date and year first above written.

BAY AREA LIBRARY AND
INFORMATION SYSTEM   CONTRACTOR

By _____   _____
Chairperson, Administrative Council

                              By_____

                              _____
                                        (Title)

                              _____

                              _____
                                      (Address)

FIGURE 4.2 — *Continued*

ADDITIONAL PROVISIONS —
BALIS STANDARD AGREEMENT

1. Contractor agrees that it is an independent Contractor and that its officers and employees do not become employees of the System nor are they entitled to any employee benefits as System Employees as a result of the execution of this agreement.

2. Contractor shall indemnify System, its officers and employees against liability for injury or damage caused by any negligent act or omission of any of its employees or volunteers or agents in the performance of this agreement and shall hold System harmless from any loss occasioned as a result of the performance of this contract by Contractor. The Contractor shall provide necessary Workman's Compensation insurance at Contractor's own cost and expense.

3. No officer, member or employee of System and no member of their governing bodies shall have any pecuniary interest, direct or indirect, in this agreement or the proceeds thereof. No employee of Contractor nor any reader of an employee's family shall serve on a System board, committee or hold any such position which either by rule, practice or action nominates, recommends supervises contractor's operations or authorizes funding to Contractor.

4. Contractor may not assign or transfer this agreement, any interest therein or claim thereunder without the prior written approval of System.

5. Payment to Contractor, will be made only upon presentation of a proper claim by Contractor subject to approval of the System Auditor Controller.

6. System shall have access to Contractor's financial records for purposes of audit. Such records shall be complete and available for audit 90 days after final payment hereunder and shall be retained and available for audit purposes for five years after final payment hereunder.

FIGURE 4.2 — *Continued*

---

7. System may terminate this agreement at any time by giving contractor a thirty (30) day written notice of such sooner termination and may be terminated at any time without notice upon a material breach of the terms of this agreement by Contractor. Contractor may terminate this agreement at any time by giving System a thirty (30) day written notice of such sooner termination.

8. Time is of the essence in each and all the provisions of this agreement.

9. No alteration or variation of the terms of this agreement shall be valid unless made in writing and signed by the parties hereto.

10. Contractor shall not be allowed or paid travel expenses unless set forth in this agreement.

11. Contractor assures that it will comply with Title VI of the Civil Rights Act of 1964 and that no person shall, on the grounds of race, creed, color, sex or national origin be excluded from participation in, be denied the benefits of, or be otherwise subjected to discrimination under this agreement.

12. System shall have a royalty-free, non-exclusive, and irrevocable license to reproduce, publish, use, and to authorize others to do so, all original computer program, writing, sound recordings, pictorial reproductions, drawings and other works of similar nature produced in the course of or under this agreement; and Contractor shall not publish any such material without prior written consent of System.

13. Contractor agrees that determinations of rights to inventions made in the course of or under this agreement shall be made by System, and that System shall acquire an irrevocable, non-exclusive, and royalty free license to practice and use, and, let any public agency practice and use, any such invention.

COMMUNITY REPRESENTATION

Select community representatives knowledgeable about youth-related issues and concerns. They should be committed to helping at-risk youth, willing to give of their time and expertise, and culturally aware and sensitive. See Figure 4.3 for a sample of community representation. For productive and manageable discussion during meetings, limit the group to a maximum of 15 people. You may make the initial recruitment for the team members by telephone, but follow up the contact with an in-person meeting. Develop a brief script detailing the purpose of the needs assessment in relation to the larger vision of the endeavor. Discuss the proposed role of the potential participant. Ask selected representatives to recommend other people for consideration. Acknowledge acceptance with a formal letter of invitation. Let the representative know the approximate length of the process, the frequency of the meetings, and major phases of the process.

Major phases of the team assessment process:

- Defining the scope of the problem
- Setting team goals, objectives, and timelines
- Assigning tasks and responsibilities
- Designing the study
- Collecting and reviewing the data
- Interpreting the data and using it to set priorities for action
- Making recommendations for policy change and/or program development
- Disseminating findings
- Evaluating program development efforts

See Chapter Three for information on how to run a meeting.

THE WORK PLAN

The work plan is a blueprint for building an adequate program or service. Figure 4.4 contains a sample timeline for a six-month process.

RESEARCH INFORMATION AND TECHNIQUES

The research method you choose to develop for the assessment of the teens depends upon several factors: What does the library need to know? How much time is required to complete the study? What are the avail-

Figure 4.3

Needs Assessment Team Representatives

- Youth representatives from local junior high and high schools
- Nonprofit sector youth-services providers (YMCA/YWCA, Boys and Girls Club, residential or out-patient adolescent mental health or substance abuse program, etc.)
- Public sector youth-service providers (recreation, child welfare, police, juvenile justice, etc.)
- School representatives (school librarian, teacher, or counselor)
- Business/corporate representatives (Chamber of Commerce, neighborhood business association); personnel officer from a local business
- Elected officials or aides
- Parent activists or child/youth advocates, PTA president or advocacy group staff)
- Local university, college, or continuing education representatives
- Leaders of local ethnic organizations representative of the target population
- Leader with grant-funding contacts

able resources? What level of expertise is available? The answers will guide you in deciding whether to collect primary data by observation or survey, or only secondary data from reports and studies. For greater credibility, gather primary data from direct observation or surveys and interviews with youth and their service providers. A combination of collection methods juxtaposes the statistical data with community members' perspectives.

Secondary Data Collection

The assessment requires demographic information (age, ethnicity, gender, family incomes) and a community profile (schools, youth resources, juvenile crime rates, employment, etc.). Answers to the following questions help to determine schedules and an available resources for at-risk teens in a specific area.

- Who provides after school development programs?
- What types of development programs exist?
- How do teens spend their time?
- Where is the time spent?

Figure 4.4
Needs Assessment Timeline

MONTH	1	2	3	4	5	6
Define scope of work	■					
Recruit advisory team		■	■			
Hire research staff (optional)	■	■	■			
Review existing reports/studies	■	■	■			
Design needs assessment				■		
Collect data				■		
Analyze findings					■	
Write report					■	■
Disseminate results						■

- How many teens are employed?
- Where are teens employed?
- What is the average income of employed teens?
- What are the rates of the leading at-risk behaviors: drug and alcohol use, school dropouts, teen pregnancy, and juvenile delinquency?

Several sources contain key demographic and economic information about teens in general, as well as specifics about at-risk teens. For example, in the Bureau of Labor Statistics there is information about teen employment rates and jobs. Census data provides information on age, gender, and language. (See Figure 4.5 for key demographic and economic information sources.)

Additional secondary sources for data collection include:

- Journals and newspaper articles
- University-based studies (and those of such foundations as the Carnegie group)
- Reports from youth advocacy organizations
- Local United Way organizations
- Local chambers of commerce
- Youth services organizations
- Churches
- Hospitals
- U.S. Department of Education of Educational Research and Improvement

Many government agencies provide statistical data via the Internet (www.fedstat.gov)

Primary Data: Observations

If the local library is near a residential area, walk through the neighborhood to see teens at work and at play. Consider walking with a teen or a youth service provider. Begin with lunch and discuss what you want to know about the community and places they think you should see.

PRIMARY DATA: SURVEYS

You make better decisions about library services and programs once you obtain and analyze the opinions, attitudes, and beliefs of at-risk youth, their providers, and library staff. These major stakeholders' suggestions and recommendations allow you to choose from a wider spectrum of achievable goals and needed programs and services. Surveys and inter-

Figure 4.5	
Needs Assessment Data Sources	
Source	**Examples of available data**
Census data	Age, gender, language, and ethnic distribution by country
Vital statistics	**Teen mortality and morbidity statistics**
Departmental data (health, social services, police, recreation, etc.)	Foster care rates, incidence of teen suicides, pregnancy, STDs, juvenile arrest
School district	**Test scores by school, school dropout rates**
Other (Bureau of Labor Statistics, city planning, state legislature, and mayoral offices, etc.)	Teen labor rates, utilization rate of teens, services
From Weisner, Stan, *Information Is Empowering*, p. 18	

views can effectively assess this group's opinions, attitudes, and beliefs about the library. Before designing the survey, you will have to make several decisions:

- What information will you use and how will it help to assess needs and develop programs?
- Will you conduct the survey with focus groups, by telephone, or in a one-on-one interview?
- Who will conduct the survey—staff, volunteers, a consultant?
- How many one-on-one interviews will you hold and who will be involved?
- What methods of evaluation and analysis do you want to use for the collected data?

Conducting numerous in-depth interviews is the ideal way to collect opinions. However, because of time and money, we often used the self-administered questionnaire. It may be necessary to use a bilingual staff member or volunteer to assist non-English-speaking participants. Figure 4.6 is a sample of a good questionnaire.

With a mailed survey, it is important to explain the need and importance of the study in a brief cover letter. You should design a user friendly, concise, brief, and easy to complete questionnaire. Do not use jargon or ask complex questions. Create a simple return process for the surveys—place in a box, leave on the desk, or provide a stamped, self-addressed envelope.

INTERVIEWING

Schedule an appointment and allow adequate time to conduct the interview. Limit the time to a maximum of 30 minutes. Stay on target, use "probes" to aid in focusing answers.

FOCUS GROUPS

It is very useful to gather a group of 6 to 12 people to discuss in detail customized library services for youth at-risk. The focus group process includes developing free-flowing open-ended questions that proceed from the general to the specific. For example:

- What are the major needs of youth at present?
- What can libraries do to support the information needs of youth, widen their perspectives, and enhance their sense of self-worth?
- What are the major needs of youth in your community?
- What can this library do to support the needs of youth in this community, needs of which they are aware and those they are not aware?

Since it is impossible to survey all of the youth and providers in a community, you will have to select a representative sample. Include in the sample a wide range of youth and their providers from varied family incomes and ethnic groups. During the focus group session, use an objective facilitator and recorder. Allow ample time for each participant's input, and state how much you value his or her opinions and experiences. Often, from the analysis of the group's exchanges, there emerges a pattern of opinions and themes that the library can use to make decisions about programs and services.

Figure 4.6

Youth Survey

WIN A DOOR PRIZE BY FILLING OUT THIS SURVEY AND RETURNING TO THE LIBRARY TABLE

**YOUTH QUESTIONNAIRE
FOR
BERKELEY CITY WIDE YOUTH FORUM
March 27, 1991**

Your Name:_____

The Berkeley Young Adult librarians would like to find out what you want from the public library. Please answer the questions below. Your participation is voluntary and your answers will be kept confidential.

1. What <u>kinds of information</u> do you feel the public libraries in Berkeley should have available for youth?

2. What <u>after school activities and programs </u>do you feel the public libraries in Berkeley should have available for youth?

3. How often do you use a public library?
   ____ at least once a week   ____ at least once a year

   ____ at least once a month   ____ almost never

4. If you currently use the library, what do you use it for? (check one or more).
   ____ taking out books/videos/tapes/records/magazines for personal use
   ____ using the equipment (copy machine, typewriter, etc.)
   ____ getting reference materials for school projects
   ____ doing your homework or completing school assignments
   ____ meeting and talking with your friends
   ____ attending a special program for youth
   ____ other _____

Figure 4.6 — *Continued*

5. What would make the library easier for you to use? (check three)
   ___ more staff to help you find things
   ___ computer catalogue instruction
   ___ more comfortable chairs/tables
   ___ greater selection of books/materials for youth
   ___ youth programs on special topics (e.g. car repair, health, careers, etc.)
   ___ other _____

6. If a youth advisory committee were available at your library, would
   you participate?
   _____Yes _____ No

7. What is the ONE thing the library could do to make you want
   to use it more often?

8. What do you think are the most important issues facing Berkeley teenagers today?
   (check three)
   ___ lack of summer jobs   ___ sexually transmitted diseases
   ___ poor schools   ___ AIDS
   ___ family problems   ___ gang violence
   ___ lack of recreation   ___ racial discrimination
   programs
   ___ drug and alcohol   ___ other_____
   abuse

Information about yourself:

School:_____ Grade:_____

Ethnic Background_____ Gender: Male_____
                                        Female_____

Thank you for your participation in the survey!!!
Make sure you hand in the completed survey at the library for your
chance at a door prize!

Data Selection

There are three ways to classify data: people, events, and things or processes. Data about people include age, gender, race, and income level. Examples of events include the number of teen pregnancies, school dropouts, and participants in after-school activities over a specified period. Data involving things include: the teen employment rate from low-income families and the number living in apartments or single-family homes. A compilation of these forms of data presents a clearer picture of at-risk youth in the library service area. With regards to employment, it is useful to know how many teens count on their jobs to contribute to family support as opposed to making personal spending money.

Bear in mind that several factors affect the data you decide to use for the assessment process. What issues about at-risk youth will you cover? On what level (local, state, or federal) is the information available? Are comparable data available for several years? How reliable are the data and the sources? What do you want to accomplish with the data? You can use data to illustrate the problem, call attention to a need, gain support for a program or service, and guide your decision as to what services to provide. At the very least, the data should compel the audience you wish to persuade to behave in a manner that supports your efforts.

You must also determine how to analyze the data, which findings to present, who should present those findings, and in what formats. It helps to consider factors such as the intended audience and the purpose for collecting the data. Shape the presentation of the findings in a manner suitable for the intended audiences—library director, staff, community groups, and the public. Remember that for some groups too many numbers and not enough anecdotes blur the message and render it ineffective.

Tips For Data Selection, Analysis, and Presentation

Gather data from official or credible sources such as the United States Census Bureau, local health and education departments, and *Kids Count Data Book*. Use the most recent available data, and verify the numbers by doublechecking as you transfer them to a report. If you did not collect the data yourself, review and understand the findings and assess what they could possibly mean for the library. Simplify the findings. Limit the use of charts, tables, and graphs. Use data that support the case the library wants to make. Create a fact sheet to highlight important information that shows the status of the at-risk teens you want to serve. Also, compare critical areas of well-being—health, delinquency, emotional development, education, and income level—of the targeted teens to

> "The thing that was so different about this was that it really focused on what were the needs of teens in our specific area."
>
> —Judy Flum[1]
>
> "Some of the things, I don't think we would have thought of without the needs assessment…so it was important, and on a larger scale, holds true for all of our libraries just in general."
>
> —Gary Morrison[2]

other youths locally or nationally. For purposes of data analysis you need to understand basic terms like average, count, mean, median, mode, rate, and ratio (see Figure 4.7).

Also, see the San Francisco Public Library needs assessment from the BALIS project in the appendix.

THE FINAL REPORT

Include all major findings in the written report. This will enable the assessment team to discuss the met and unmet needs; highlight any barriers to library use, physical as well as psychological; and determine gaps in library services and programs to this group. It may also identify the need to develop or modify some library policies and procedures. The sample outline in Figure 4.8 is a guide for completion of the final report.

Figure 4.7

Terms Used in Data Analysis

- AVERAGE A number that refers to the "middle" of the group, or what is "typical."

- COUNT The actual number (i.e., the number of teens in tenth grade in the state).

- MEAN A type of average. Example: a total of 100 (hundred) teens in the targeted area is employed; the total annual income of those 100 teens is $30,000 (thousand); the average (mean) annual income of the teens is $300 (hundred). The total number of teens (100) is divided by the total annual salary of the teens ($30,000). (100 ÷ 30,000 = 300)

- MEDIAN A type of average that divides a group of numbers into equal halves. The numbers are listed from the smallest to the largest, or vice versa. Example: if the median reading level of 15-year-old teens in the area is seventh grade, this means half the teens in the area read below the seventh grade level, and the other half read above the level.

- MODE Another type of average that is determined by the number or range of numbers in a set that occurs most frequently. Example: If the mode age of teen graduates from high school is 18, then this means that more teens finished high school at age 18 than at any other age.

- RATE Measures a part (the subgroup), relates it to the whole (total group), and uses a base (the multiplier) of per 100 (or per 1,000, or per 100,000 depending on the size of the group). Example: Using a base of per 100, a total of 1,500 (hundred) teens entered the twelfth grade in the area during the 1998/99 school year; 400 (hundred) of those teens graduated during the 1998/99 school year; the graduation rate was then 22.6% One could then say, approximately 27 (rounded) out of every 100 teens graduated. (400 ÷ 1500 = .2666 × 100 = 26.6)

- RATIO Measures the relationship between two numbers (e.g., how much bigger or smaller a number is compared to the other). Example: If the graduation rate at Dulaney High for the 1999 senior class was 35.9 per 100 students, and at Long Beach High the graduation rate for the senior class of 1999 was 22.6 per 100 students, the graduation ratio between the two schools for 1999 would have been 1.6 with Dulaney Valley having the higher ratio. (35.9 ÷ 22.6 = 1.58 (1.6 rounded))

Figure 4.8

Needs Assessment Report Outline

   I. Executive summary
  II. Introduction
     A. Purpose of project—YA Services and YAR
     B. Sites for study
     C. Guidelines/parameters of project
  III. Design
     A. Provider survey
     B. Demographics/social indicators
     C. Interviews/focus groups
     D. Other reports/data sources
  IV. Description of community context for youth
     A. Demographics—population, neighborhood, ethnicity, etc.
     B. Schools
     C. Major organizations/agencies—network of services
   V. Key Indicators of status of youth—Current trends
     A. Youth employment
     B. Health/mental health
     C. Substance abuse
     D. Child welfare
     E. Juvenile justice
     F. School performance
  VI. Major problems/Unmet needs (provider survey and interviews)
     A. Problems (as perceived by youth and adults)
     B. Unmet needs—prioritized
 VII. YA services ideas/proposals
     A. Collaborative projects
     B. New or expanded programs
     C. Outreach strategies
     D. Neighborhood branch/population—focused services
VIII. Implementation plan/recommendations
     A. Timetable
     B. Key participants

BROAD ASSESSMENT FINDINGS FROM THE BAY AREA PROJECT

As mentioned earlier, each of the BALIS participating libraries needs assessments revealed that libraries had to do a much better job of reaching out not only to youth, but also to those serving youth in the communities. There were some noteworthy common threads in their findings:

- African Americans as a group, but especially males, were at the greatest risk.
- The top five areas of concern were family instability, substance abuse, limited economic opportunities, low rate of educational success, and need for interpersonal support.
- Ways that both teens and their service providers recommended to serve this group better included community outreach, forums to address issues and concerns, tutoring and homework help, job skills training, and forming stronger links with community-based organizations.
- Barriers to attracting these teens to the library were their perceptions of the library as being too structured, stuffy, quiet, boring, and too academic.

REFERENCES

1.   Judy Flum, Interview with the author, October 1995.
2.   Gary Morrison, Interview with the author, October 1995.

Chapter 5

Are We There Yet? Planning and Evaluation

PLANNING

The planning process begins with deciding whom to involve, determining what is required to complete the effort, and then writing the planning document. First, you must analyze the staff's capability and readiness to develop and implement additional services and programs. This is critical because implementing new services and programs require strengthened support at several levels. Particularly in large systems, a comprehensive review of all current library activities and plans helps to avoid conflicting or competing timelines during the implementation phase of your project. As mentioned in Chapter Three, the book entitled *Planning for Results: A Public Library Transformation Process*[1] is a helpful guide.

Planning allows you to establish clear goals, develop achievable objectives, determine needed resources and funding, and set a timetable for implementation and completion of strategies. A **goal** is a broad, long-range statement of what you want to accomplish, for example: to find, attract, and serve at-risk youth. An **objective** is a measurable action toward accomplishing the goal, for example: by December of 2002, we will develop and implement a job information center for at-risk teens. Second, we expect to serve a minimum of 50 teens per month by April 2003. A **strategy** is the method or steps taken to implement the objective, for example: purchase books and pamphlets on various jobs available to teens, and provide attentive expert assistance.

The written plan includes an executive summary; the mission and vi-

Figure 5.1

Written Plan Checklist

Executive Summary
- Summarizes the major components of the plan. Includes
- Library's name, mission, and vision.
- Information about the at-risk population and their needs.
- What services or programs you will provide and how they will address the identified needs.
- Your capacity to deliver the service or program.
- Goals, objectives, and evaluation.
- Budget.
- Program continuation after the initial funding period.

Mission
- Simply states the purpose for your library's existence.

Vision
- States what will happen if the mission is carried forth, in this case specifically for at-risk youth.

Needs Statement
- Key findings from the needs assessment are listed.

Program Goals
- Broad statement of what you want to accomplish.

Objectives
- Specific steps toward achievement of goals.

Evaluation
- Answers when and how the library knows it has achieved success as stated in its goals and objectives. Choose measures of success that can be measured accurately and annually, rather than overly "ambitious" long-term hard-to-measure objectives.

Budget
- The budget will cover cost for: salaries and benefits, library materials, supplies, equipment, training, public relations, etc.

sion of the library; a list of goals, objectives and strategies; and the budget. The plan should support the mission of the library as well as relate to the unmet needs of youth as determined by the needs assessment. In the case of the budget, it may require reallocating current funding or finding new funding. At any rate, it is essential to include a detailed listing of the amount of money and other required resources necessary to realize the plan. If planning a budget is too much of a fiscal challenge for you, seek the assistance of a knowledgeable staff member or the expertise of one of the members of the assessment team. Figure 5.1 is a checklist for the written plan. Remember, a well-crafted plan keeps you focused on the necessary tasks and mindful of the timeline while implementing your services and programs. Finally, so that the public and the assessment participants have a sense of how their efforts contributed to the service delivery plan, you should excerpt and publicize major planning initiatives. You can accomplish this with a featured newspaper article in the local paper and in a follow-up thank-you letter to the assessment team.

THE PLANS: TEENS JOBS TO TUTORING

The nine BALIS libraries developed a variety of initiatives to address the needs of teens in each of the service areas. *Excellence in Library Services to Young Adults*[2] featured the Alameda County Public Library's multifaceted outreach project held through the San Lorenzo Branch. It also included two projects from the Berkeley Public Library: in-service training day and employing young adults in the library. Quotes are from staff members involved with the programs discussed below.

Alameda County Public Library—San Lorenzo Branch

> We at San Lorenzo were surprised at the range of costs of the programs. We had a budget of $500 for each program. We found some we could do free. Others cost $1,000; that was an education.
> —Gary Morris

The major need of teens in San Lorenzo were for information directly related to jobs and job skills, multicultural relations, health and sexuality, and awareness of youth-related community and library resources. These identified needs guided the plans of the San Lorenzo staff. They decided to take a multifaceted approach to respond to the targeted group of teens. Additional needs included family stability, community recreation programs, and youth facilities.

Members of the steering committee, comprised of youth and their service providers, developed four goals:

1. To increase youth awareness of library resources.
2. To provide interactive, informational forums for young adults that address the key issues identified in the needs assessment.
3. To increase understanding and communication between library staff and community young adults.
4. To work cooperatively with community organizations and agencies to heighten awareness of youths at-risk issues.

The planning group decided to hold seven youth forums to address an array of topics ranging from job opportunities, interviewing skills, cultural sensitivity, sexuality, and relationships to a "rap against racism." The teens and staff developed and distributed two informational brochures: "For Y.A.s Only!" and "Young Adult Resources Guide: San Lorenzo Area." The "For YAs Only!" brochure highlighted young adult and general library programs and services. The brochure provided information about library hours, directions to getting to the branch, loan periods, types of materials, and how to get a library card. The "Young Adult Resources Guide: San Lorenzo Area" listed the names and telephone numbers of 24-hour crisis lines, child care referral agencies, gay and lesbian youth agencies, schools, and job training opportunities.

This total project cost $67,545.

BUDGET DETAILS

Revenues

LSCA Grant	$37,710
In-kind Contribution (donated by the library)	29,835
Total	$67,545

Expenses

Printing and duplication	$ 1,975
Library materials	11,300
Contractual personnel	3,500
Equipment	1,500
Refreshments	400
Salaries	19,035
Subtotal	$37,710
Library Services	$29,835
Total	$67,545

Berkeley Public Library

> *What we were not acutely aware of was that their [at-risk youth]*
> *number one concern in this city is work/jobs.*
>
> —Regina Minudri

In response to needs assessment findings that they needed to address employment among multicultural teens, and information about library services, Berkeley Public Library developed three goals:

1. To reach out to the multicultural youth community through four youth initiated programs and five library displays highlighting cultural diversity.
2. To provide employment opportunities that develop confidence and job skills.
3. To improve young adult collections in the areas of health and mental health.

Objectives relating to the goals ranged from installing cultural diversity displays and developing student worker job descriptions to purchasing books, pamphlets, and videos on the subject of health and mental health issues affecting teenagers. Their two major initiatives, the in-service training day and the employment of at-risk youth, contributed immensely to the lasting legacy of the BALIS project.

IN-SERVICE STAFF DAY

A young adult librarian suggested that an in-service day take place so that all staff could learn about teen behavioral issues and the potential role the library could play in the lives of teens. With the library system closed for the entire morning, staff received four hours of training related to the physical aspects of adolescence, the social world of youth, and the political tensions between the library and teens. Several professionals addressed teen issues including a nurse practitioner in adolescent medicine, a city high school curriculum developer, and the lead teacher of a multicultural studies course. The outcomes of the day resulted in raised levels of consciousness, comfort, and sensitivity. The library director's discretionary fund paid for the event.

BUDGET

Revenues

Director's discretionary fund	$2,595

Expenses

Speakers	$ 925
T-shirts	1,400
Refreshments	160
Paper goods	30
Staff equipment setup	80
Total	$2,595

YOUNG ADULT EMPLOYMENT

Getting a job was the number one concern for Berkeley's youth. Three teens hired by the library for three locations designed programs and advised youth librarians on issues of library services for their peers. The teen employees received public service orientation, performed outreach and clerical work, and developed computer literacy skills. Initially, the library paid $5,000 for the teens' salaries; eventually, the success of the program resulted in the creation of three permanent student positions.

Alameda Free Library

Because Alameda teens' number one concern emerged as that of succeeding in school, the library responded by developing the following goals:

1. To improve awareness and visibility of the library and the services it has to offer.
2. To improve availability of and access to a greater variety of materials for young adults.
3. To act as a clearinghouse for tutors.
4. To improve library service to the community and youth at risk by working together with other community service providers.

"Taking the regional approach added to the richness . . . and made the project unusual."

—Judy Flum

Initiatives to accomplish the goal of raising awareness and visibility of the library included developing and disseminating thousands of book covers to middle school and high school aged students in Alameda. To achieve the goal of improving availability of and access to a greater variety of materials, the library planned to make several changes:

1. Make accessible a resource/referral binder on teen issues and available community resources.
2. Review library policies regarding the minimum age for video borrowing privileges.
3. Increase the allocation for young adult materials by 50 percent.
4. Plan and conduct an annual program for youth.
5. Relocate and expand the young adult area in the main library.

In order to serve as a clearinghouse for tutors assisting young people with their homework, the library planned a series of activities over a three-month period. They planned to select a program coordinator who was expected to contact various community agencies and schools to recruit tutors, and then publicize the new program in schools and throughout the community.

The library developed five objectives to support their goal to improve library services to the community and youth at risk by working together with other community service providers. They were as follows:

1. Contact Xanthos, Inc. for their list of recommended reading to add to the public library circulating collections.
2. Develop a plan for public library-school coordinated support services with appropriate school representatives.
3. Investigate the feasibility of creating a youth advisory team to work in conjunction with the library project team.
4. Update the resource/referral binder on a quarterly basis.
5. Send at least one library representative to the quarterly meetings of the Alameda Youth Activities Network.

The budget to implement the proposed plans included use of existing staff and facilities plus a $23,618 request for programming.

Contra Costa County Library

The Contra Costa County assessment found that teens "lacked information on youth services, a lack of coordination among youth serving agencies, and lack of outreach by the library to agencies."[3] The San Pablo

Branch of the Contra Costa County Library developed four goals to address the findings:

1. To improve library service to community-based organizations serving youth at risk.
2. To improve outreach services to at-risk youth in community-based organizations.
3. To contribute to cultural awareness and acceptance of differences among youth in the community.
4. To increase networking between community-based organizations serving youth and local libraries.

To support the first goal of improving library service to community-based organizations serving youth at risk, the library planned to build a video collection to use to start group discussion on life issues facing youth at risk. They also planned to make the collection accessible to organizations and individuals. The collection would be augmented with materials in other formats such as pamphlets, paperbacks, comic books, and so forth.

As a means to improve outreach services to at-risk youth in community-based organizations, the library planned to target 25 boys and girls in grades six through eight in the Asian Youth Group at a local junior high school. They would provide support materials for discussion sessions on life issues and create special programming that included Asian storytelling and dancing. They also planned to provide materials to the group with support for homework help and to teach library access skills.

To accomplish the goal of contributing to cultural awareness and acceptance of difference among youth in the community, plans were made to develop and implement two Asian programs. Plans for the fourth goal—to increase networking between community-based organizations serving youth and local libraries—included partnering with the Richmond Pubic Library. The two libraries coordinated plans and implementation of four meetings with several community-based organizations, alternating between the two locations.

Hayward Public Library

The young people of Hayward needed ongoing services to deal with the everyday obstacles they faced. The goal was to provide for the informational needs of the youth of Hayward in particular day-to-day living skills. The library staff planned to feature speakers who would discuss a series of practical topics related to the teens' expressed issues and concerns.

Topics included "Finding and Holding a Job" and "Staying Free of Drugs." They also planned to compile and distribute a resource guide for teens and gather and distribute pamphlets of interest to youth.

Livermore Public Library

Doing well in school concerned the youth of Livermore. The staff learned that teens were confused about library policies, unaware of the existing young adult area, and uncomfortable with the public access catalog. To help meet the needs of the youth of Livermore, the library developed five goals:

1. To improve the youths and provide access to referral information by producing the *Unhappy at Home?* booklet.
2. To improve youth knowledge of and access to library services and materials through collaborative outreach projects.
3. To expand the young adult paperback collection and increase its use.
4. To provide youth employment training and opportunities.
5. To improve library services to youth by responding to concerns expressed in the "Livermore Youth at Risk Report."

In support of the goal to improve youths and provide access to referral information, plans were made to develop and disseminate the *Unhappy at Home?* booklet. As part of accomplishing the goal of improving youth knowledge, plans were developed for implementation of outreach projects for middle and high school students that included a video, bookmarks, and articles for the school newspaper. Additional funding, booklists, and better signage were planned to accomplish the goal of expanding and increasing use of the young adult paperback collection. Several initiatives were developed to support the goal of providing youth employment training and opportunities. Library staff decided to create more hours for high school student pages and to develop and implement at least one program on finding employment, including developing interview skills.

In an effort to address those concerns that teen had about the library, staff planned to review the library policies that required parental signatures for library cards. They also agreed to conduct one all-staff training session to review several elements of the library services affecting young people, and develop procedures for effective ways of working with them. The budget request for the project was $19,643.

Oakland Public Library

The high school dropout rate and poor performance indicators among the youth of Oakland motivated Oakland Public Library to create a homework/tutorial center in the Martin Luther King Jr. Branch. They established two goals:

1. To offer homework and tutorial support to seventh- through ninth-grade students so that they could increase their confidence in their study skills, improve their academic achievement and, thereby, prepare themselves to lead lives that are more productive.
2. To build a coalition between Oakland Public Library and community agencies providing tutorial services to young adults within the Martin Luther King Jr. Branch neighborhood and citywide.

The plans to offer homework and tutorial support included recruitment and training of at least 12 tutors and publicity to attract students. To build a coalition between Oakland Public Library and community agencies, staff determined that they needed to identify agencies offering tutorial services and explore the feasibility of sharing tutorial resources with existing agencies and establishing off-site tutorial centers.

Richmond Public Library

In response to the limited literacy skills and the high dropout rate among Richmond's teens, the library chose to enhance and expand its TLC (Tutoring Library Connection) service plan. The goal of the new TLC service plan was to improve the educational success of young people by supplementing the formal tutoring efforts of community-based organizations. The planned activities included use of the MOP (Mobile Outreach Program) van for monthly visits to community-based organization sites to issue library cards, discuss library services, and give book talks. They also planned to provide specialized bibliographies, disseminate information about local educational and cultural events of interest to youth, conduct library tours, and give bibliographic instruction. Overall, the program was designed to encourage youth between the ages of 14 and 18 to stay in and succeed in school. The total projected budget was $15,713.

San Francisco Public Library

The findings confirmed that the teens most at-risk were African-American youth, particularly males, followed by Latino youth and those with limited English proficiency. In part because of this information, the San Francisco Public Library chose to implement projects at three branch locations—Bayview/Hunters Point, the Excelsior, and the Tenderloin. The Young Adult Planning Committee drafted a mission statement: "San Francisco Public Library's Young Adult Services mission is to provide and promote library services and materials relevant to the unique recreational and informational needs of the city's diverse adolescent population, aged 13-18, supporting their transition from childhood into adulthood, and encouraging their lifelong use of libraries." To achieve their mission, they developed four goals and several objectives:

1. To revise current library policies, services, and procedures to remove barriers to serving youth at-risk.
2. To develop a model for focused library services for youth at risk at branch libraries, working in partnership with community agencies and schools.
3. To create a model for providing off-site services designed to reach youth at risk.
4. To create a targeted publicity campaign to promote library use by youth at risk.

To support their goal of removing barriers for teens, staff made plans to examine current policies, procedures, and services. Librarians at the Bayview/Anna E. Waden Branch would be selected to create a model for focused library services at the branch libraries. They were expected to create a teen corner, expand the young adult collection, and work with schools and other community groups to enhance services for area teens.

Plans to implement a model for off-site services designed to reach teens involved a librarian, the Youth-at-Risk Planning Committee, and the Youth Guidance Center staff. The librarian working with the project would be required to develop policies, procedures, and services for an off-site library program at the Youth Guidance Center. Publicity campaign initiatives included radio and television public service announcements (PSAs), and posters and flyers.

EVALUATION

> *Evaluating programs is very difficult . . . It's a very inexact exercise,
> the threshold question is: What we want to know about a program,
> is it knowable? Sometime it isn't, sometimes it is, sometimes what's
> knowable isn't useful, sometimes what's useful isn't knowable.*
> —Timothy D. Armbruster, former executive director,
> Morris Goldseker Foundation

Selected Evaluation Methods

Each of the participating BALIS libraries chose a variety of standards and methods to determine how successful it was at accomplishing its goals and objectives.

ALAMEDA COUNTY LIBRARY

To measure the affect of the program on youth, the San Lorenzo Library used program attendance and evaluations and material circulation. They also used statistics on questions asked and answered at the "Stump the Librarian" booth, young adult library card use, evaluations by a youth panel, and the Youth at Risk Steering Committee. Another measure was the feedback from the informational brochures.

BERKELEY PUBLIC LIBRARY

The Berkeley Public Library decided to have young adult librarians conduct formal quarterly evaluations to measure the effectiveness of their programs, employment of youth, and outreach. The librarians had to complete four programs, noting attendance, and monitor the progress and attendance of the three hired students. They also had to log contacts, outreach visits, class visits, booktalks, and to measure cooperation with other local agencies.

OAKLAND PUBLIC LIBRARY

Oakland Public Library's criteria for evaluating the tutorial/homework center focused on data collected from teachers, tutors, and students associated with the program. Baseline data for each student's school grades and attendance were established and compared with grades after three months in the program.

SAN FRANCISCO PUBLIC LIBRARY

To measure how well the San Francisco Public Library met the educational and informational needs of youth at risk they chose to track circulation statistics for young adult collections. The library staff also:

1. Sampled semiannually branch use by youth at the Bayview/Anna E. Waden Branch.
2. Monitored materials borrowed at the Youth Guidance Center.
3. Surveyed staff at both the Youth Guidance and Woodside Learning Centers semiannually.

The Evaluation Process

For several reasons, evaluation is a critical component of the planning process. First, creating a method to evaluate your plan of action helps to clarify objectives. Second, it makes it possible to measure progress toward achievement of your objectives. Third, a good evaluation method makes it possible to develop an appropriate rationale for sustaining, expanding, modifying, or eliminating a project. Fourth, a positive evaluation serves as a marketing opportunity to motivate others to support your efforts. Finally, an evaluation aids and encourages others to implement similar programs by learning from your success or failure.

Decide who should conduct the evaluation—staff or an outsider. If you choose an outside evaluator, consider fees, credibility, and the level of involvement needed for the evaluation design. For a staff evaluator, you must also consider the cost in staff time, the staff member's ability to perform a credible evaluation, and the staff member's level of objectivity. Remember that for comparative purposes, collect appropriate data before the beginning of the project. For example, if you wish to increase library use by teens, sample use by teens before the project begins so that you can fairly assess if your efforts have contributed to greater use. Review *Output Measures and More: Planning and Evaluating Public Library Services for Young Adults.*[4] This is an excellent source for additional information and forms needed for obtaining samples.

Evaluation Design

The elements of evaluation include inputs, outputs, and outcomes. "Desired outcomes of a service will tend to relate to long-term social, behavioral, or even economic objectives that are rather intangible." " . . . Long-term objectives should provide the justification for the existence of a service, yet it is virtually impossible to measure the degree to which they are achieved."[5]

The evaluation criteria should relate to the output level. For example, in addressing the issue of school dropouts, you may have developed a homework tutorial program for middle school youth. Short of a long-term longitudinal study, it is difficult to determine if the tutoring received by an at-risk student prevented him/her from dropping out and enabled him/her to complete high school. However, it is possible to determine how many of those students participated in the homework tutorial program, and whether their grades and, most important, their attitudes toward learning improved within a specific period.

An evaluation considers both the quantitative and the qualitative aspects of an initiative. Quantitative aspects involve hard measurement and the qualitative deal with the narrative or anecdotal accounts. A good evaluation requires a great deal of preliminary thinking and work.

- What are important factors to evaluate?
- What will success look like? What is measurable?
- Who needs the data for decision making/funding/improvement?
- Is there a buy-in as to the credibility or acceptance of the success indicators? By whom?
- Can other libraries serve as models?
- What will it take to reach the desired outcome? (For example, in order to heighten awareness of teen services it will cost $3,000 to develop and distribute brochures and create a series of informative programs).

The evaluation needs to incorporate all of those factors necessary to persuade the stakeholders to continue to support and fund a project.

QUANTITATIVE EVALUATION

While numbers demonstrate accountability, here you must be careful to avoid confusing large numbers of participants as the total indicator of a successful program or service. On the surface, reaching 1,800 young people sounds much more successful than reaching three. However, a high number versus a low number does not always tell the whole story. A case in point is that of the three students employed at the Berkeley Public Library versus the distribution of thousands of hip-pocket brochures by libraries in Contra Costa and Richmond. Nevertheless, from the beginning, it is important to convey to those who will decide the fate of the project how you designated a certain target number to measure success. Often with creating innovative programs and services there is little baseline data to use as a realistic gauge for setting appropriate targets, so you may want to begin with conservative figures and modify them if necessary.

QUALITATIVE EVALUATION

"Sometimes the story of one individual whose life was changed through an interaction with a library is worth more than any number of output measures."[6] Share the positive experiences of your program's participants. This will provide memorable, visual examples that will allow key stakeholders and supporters to easily remember and discuss your project with others. In addition to the quantitative data, recording the "small victories and tender triumphs"[7] will add real meaning to your statistical reports. Let your teens know at the beginning of your program or new service how much you value their opinions, and how important it is for them to evaluate the project.

EVALUATION GUIDE

- Use clear, credible, and measurable objectives.
- Know who will review the results.
- Evaluate both the process and the results; separate the two but show their relationship to each other.
- Decide who should conduct the evaluation—staff or outsider.
- Decide the method of analyzing the collected data.
- Determine who will present the data.
- Decide the method of analyzing the collected data.
- Determine who will present the data.
- Understand generally how the overall performance of the library is measured.

Whether you choose to use a combination of qualitative and quantitative data, it is important that your evaluation report be timely. You may find it helpful to develop an abridged "public" report that highlights the critical areas of your initiatives.

A library may offer various programs that are beyond the scope of "traditional" services. Each one presents a different problem for evaluation. The library needs to be evaluated not only in terms of "how is it doing" but also in terms of "is it doing what it should be doing?"

Libraries can offer various programs that are beyond the scope of "traditional" services. Each one presents a different problem for evaluation.

REFERENCES

1. Ethel E. Himmel and William James Wilson, *Planning for Results: A Public Library Transformation Process* (Chicago: American Library Association, 1998).
2. Mary K. Chelton, ed., *Excellence in Library Services to Young Adults* (Chicago: American Library Association, 1994), 1–4.
3. Stan Weisner, *Information Is Empowering: Developing Public Library Services for Youth-at-Risk* (Oakland: GRT Book Printing, 1992).
4. Virginia A. Walter, *Output Measures and More: Planning and Evaluation Public Library Services for Young Adults* (Chicago: American Library Association, 1995).
5. F. W. Lancaster, *If You Evaluate Your Library*, 2d. ed. (Champaign: University of Illinois, 1993), 17.
6. Walter, 31.
7. Walter, 31.

Chapter 6

Money Talk: Grants and Gifts

Ask and it shall be given?

The United States has no shortage of programs or foundation money. We are woefully behind in conceptualizing what it is about the programs that work. We have effective programs. What we do not have is a solid system for assessing, improving, sustaining, and expanding their impact.

—Karen J. Pittman, Director
International Youth Foundation

Lack of money should not prevent you from implementing a service or an innovative program for at-risk teens. There are foundations with billions of dollars in assets that annually grant millions of dollars to support thousands of programs and services for all of mankind. The top 100 foundations and audited financial data can be found at <www. fdnceter. org/grantmaker/trends/top100giving.html>. Frequently, their funding enhances activities that tend to "carry public policy in new and uncharted directions to benefit the whole of society."[1] F. Emerson Andrews describes a foundation as: "nongovernmental, nonprofit, has principal fund of its own, is managed by its own trustees and directors. Is established to maintain or aid social, educational, charitable, religious, or other activities serving the common welfare."[2] While grants are becoming a larger part of library support, librarians, particularly those of us in youth services, do not yet use corporate and foundation funding enough for our new initiatives. On the other hand, Steele and Elder, in their book *Becoming a Fundraiser* note that while there is a great deal of available money, in most cases it takes tremendous effort and time to obtain foundation and corporate funding. Foundation and corporate gifts are not the "open-to-all-comers, all-it-takes-is-a-good-proposal" affairs some think them to be.[3] More often, the receipt of a large foundation grant or corporate gift comes as the result of long-term cultivation, and involves advance meetings with a program officer from a foundation or corporation who has an interest in your mission. "The worst way to go about raising money from foundations and corporations is to read about them and send them proposals out of the blue with no champion to back them within the organization."[4] In addition, the proposal should demonstrate its relationship to the foundation's priorities. Corporations normally give away money because there is something in it for them, ("enlightened self interest").[5] One of the most important self-serving investments they can make to a community is funding services to children and youth, especially to those with the fewest opportunities.

Despite the challenges, opportunities abound for librarians who choose to compete aggressively for private and public grant dollars. The pursuit of funding for at-risk teen projects is less difficult if you have completed a thorough youth needs assessment (see Chapter Five). That assessment will help you present a clear vision of what needs to happen for your clientele and show in a compelling fashion how it is related to social and economic priorities on both local and global levels. Next, you should outline how the library intends to fulfil its role in providing the service or program and share the expected pay-off with society. The library needs a sound policy and procedures detailing how it will accept grants, gifts, and donations (see Figure 6.1).

THE PROPOSAL

"Come up with a good idea that solves a problem, serves people or serves a community, that can be evaluated for its effectiveness, and that has replications potential for other communities."[6] Replication potential is extraordinarily important to most foundations, and a well-written proposal increases the likelihood that a project will receive careful consideration.

Figure 6.1

Contribution and Donation Acceptance Policy

THE COMMUNITY FREE LIBRARY

POLICY

SUBJECT: CONTRIBUTION AND DONATION ACCEPTANCE

The Community Free Library welcomes and invites financial support. The following gift types are acceptable at this time:

Cash
Securities
Stock
Bequests
Life Insurance

Gifts of real and personal property will be considered on a case-by-case basis at the discretion of the Director and Board of Trustees.

The Library will accept gifts that are restricted by donors, provided the nature of the restriction is consistent with the Library's overall programs and services. Donor restrictions will be stated in writing.

POLICY

SUBJECT: GRANTS

The Community Free Library is open to opportunities for grants from public and private sources. Staff are encouraged to be on the lookout for such opportunities and to advise the appropriate staff. Further, staff are encouraged to participate in the development and conception of grant-supported programs.

All grant applications are to be submitted under the signature of the Director of the Library.

Eight Basic Steps

There are eight basic steps in proposal writing.

1. Study the priority areas of interest set forth by the foundation or agency carefully. Your proposal must fit their profile.
2. Identify a problem or need that describes an existing adverse condition and requires corrective action.
3. Establish measurable program objectives that describe the outcome of the program or project.
4. Define methods to use in order to meet the objectives and clearly describe the program activities.
5. Describe the methods that will be used to evaluate the program.
6. Develop a time line. Consider structuring the proposal in phases, with each successive phase building on the previous one.
7. List the individual and the agency responsible for the activity.
8. Establish a budget to reflect adequate funding.

Parts of the Proposal

The proposal has eight major parts.

1. Summary or executive abstract
2. Introduction
3. Problem statement/needs assessment
4. Program objectives
5. Methods
6. Evaluation
7. Account of other necessary funding
8. Budget

SUMMARY CHECKLIST

- Belongs at the beginning of the proposal
- Identifies the grant applicant
- Includes at least one sentence about credibility
- Includes at least one sentence about the problem
- Includes at least one sentence about methods
- Includes project's total cost, including value of in-kind contributions and funds already obtained
- Is brief
- Is clear
- Is interesting

Although the summary appears at the beginning of the proposal, it is better to prepare it after the proposal is completed. Do devote time to the development of a concise and comprehensive summary because it will set the tone for the rest of the proposal.

INTRODUCTION

- Clearly establishes who is applying for funds
- Describes the agency's overall purpose and goals
- Describes the agency's programs
- Describes clients or constituents
- Provides evidence of previous accomplishments
- Offers statistics to support credibility
- Offers statements and /or endorsements to support credibility
- Supports credibility in program area in which funds are sought
- Describes relevance of project to larger issues
- Leads logically to problem statements
- Demonstrates collaborative efforts with other agencies serving the targeted audience
- Is interesting
- Is free of jargon
- Is brief

A comprehensive introduction establishes the agency's credibility for receipt of funding.

PROBLEM STATEMENT/NEEDS ASSESSMENT

- Relates to purposes and goals of the organization
- Is of reasonable dimensions
- Provides supporting statements from authorities
- States problem in terms of clients or beneficiaries
- Is developed with input from clients and beneficiaries
- Makes no assumptions
- Uses no jargon
- Is interesting to read

The problem statement/needs assessment portion of the proposal makes the case or rationale for the importance of providing funds for the project.

Program Objectives

- Describes problem-related outcomes of your program
- Does not describe methods
- Defines the population served
- States objective timeline
- Describes the objectives in numerical terms

A description of the program objectives explains what the library intends to accomplish.

Description of Methods

- Flows naturally from problems and objectives
- Clearly describes program activities
- States reasons for selection of activities
- Describes sequence of activities
- Describes staffing of program, especially staff training
- Describes clients and client selection
- Presents a reasonable scope of activities to accomplish within the time allotted for programs and within the resources of the applicant

Describe the methods in terms of the actions the library intends to follow to achieve the desired results.

The Evaluation

- Covers product and process—what and how
- Tells who performs the evaluation as well as describes the evaluator selection process
- Defines the evaluation criteria
- Describes data gathering methods
- Explains the use of any test instruments or questionnaires
- Describes the process of data analysis
- Shows how the evaluation process will improve the program
- Describes the elements of the evaluation reports

A good evaluation method helps you focus on your objectives and, where possible, not only emphasizes the number of participants and other statistics, but also shows evidence of trying to measure changes in attitude, behavior, and performance.

> "We have such simplistic negative answers in the United States. We have a pregnancy problem—give them contraceptives. We have a violent kid—make them trade their guns for shoes. Instead, we should start with the positive, help children become something, not just stop doing something."
>
> —Karen J. Pittman[7]

ACCOUNT OF OTHER NECESSARY FUNDING

- Presents a future-funding plan
- Discusses both maintenance and future program funding if there will be construction
- Accounts for other needed expenditures (e.g., insurance, maintenance, and repairs) when the program includes equipment purchases
- Shows effort to encourage replication of the project

This important part of the proposal explains where the library plans to obtain the necessary funding for the project beyond the grant period. Consideration for future funding of a project needs to occur within the context of the library's overall financial projections and plans. The library may be able to assume future fiscal responsibility of a successful project and include the expense in its budget request at the end of the grant period. A financial partnership with another youth-serving agency or a fundraising effort may also provide future alternative funding for your project. A full accounting as to how you will integrate a much-needed project into your services on a long-term basis significantly enhances your proposal.

THE BUDGET

- Includes all personnel costs
- Includes all nonpersonnel costs
- Provides a financial summary

This section provides detailed estimates of the anticipated costs for the program or service. It is beneficial to provide budget details for every aspect of the project as well as to prepare a good summary.

A WHOLE NEW WORLD

In April 1995, the Enoch Pratt Free Library in Baltimore, Maryland, implemented "A Whole New World," an electronic literacy demonstration project. The project provided Internet training for at-risk youth between the ages of 9 and 14. While the library was fortunate to receive the seed money to create "A Whole New World," it had to compete aggressively for grant and private monies in order to expand the program to additional sites. The following proposal serves as a guide for writing a proposal.

Grant Proposal

Introduction and Organization Information
Mission
The mission of the Enoch Pratt Free Library is to provide access to information resources, staff, facilities, and services that respond to the pursuit of knowledge, education, lifelong learning opportunities, and cultural enrichment by the people of the City of Baltimore and other residents of the State of Maryland.

Goals
The Strategic Plan for the Enoch Pratt Free Library lists the following goals for achieving excellence:
- establishing an atmosphere for external and internal customers that encourages learning
- employing the best technological tools available to provide a variety of services and programs to its customers
- building on the best of Pratt's past in designing future programs
- exploring and creating partnerships and other opportunities to maximize and/or expand the Library's resources
- valuing diversity in the work force and customer base
- providing management and staff with equal access to advancement opportunities as well as the training and tools they need to achieve the Library's goals and their own professional aims
- aligning the Library's systems and structures to support these goals and to ensure organizational effectiveness

Current Programs and Activities
Using a community based system of branches, a Central Library equipped for reference and research, bookmobiles for children and adults, deposit collections, and computer connections, the Enoch Pratt Free Library serves the diverse needs of a city of neighborhoods, and the entire state of Maryland through a variety of programs and services.

On a grassroots level, the branch libraries serve as gathering places for the communities and families to visit and enjoy together; homework helpers for children; meeting places for neighborhood organizations; and centers for education, information, and recreation for citizens of all ages. The Pratt Central Children's Department,

Grant Proposal — *Continued*

along with children's sections of our branch libraries, continue to provide special programming for our youngest customers through story hours, puppet shows, film screenings and a summer reading program. In addition, the Pratt Central Library recently opened a new educational center for young people called "Student Express," a service designed to assist students with school work, career guidance, college preparation, and recreational reading. Similarly, the neighborhood branches have set up Student Study Centers where students will find educational materials that aid them in their schoolwork and college preparation.

The Pratt Library is also playing a pivotal role in providing information through technology in Baltimore City, the State of Maryland and throughout the country. Pratt was the first public library in Maryland to offer public access to the Internet. Through information technology, Pratt serves as an Internet gateway for Baltimore City government officials, Maryland State Archives, and Sailor, the state online public information network.

Community-Based Organization
In addition to the 28 branches dedicated to neighborhoods throughout the city, the Enoch Pratt Library is an active contributor to the revitalization of city neighborhoods benefiting from the federal Empowerment Zone grant awarded to Baltimore. Involved in the planning from the moment the grant proposal began taking shape, Pratt has been asked to play a variety of roles in the grant implementation over the next four years. An introductory series of community information programs on basic topics such as housing, jobs, and small business economic planning, was presented by the Library in cooperation with the Empower Baltimore Management Corporation. As plans develop, "Village Centers" in each Empowerment Zone community will be connected electronically with Pratt's information resources. In the meantime, information on the grant and its implications is provided at all Pratt public service agencies.

Relationship with Proposed Program Sites
The Brooklyn and Pennsylvania Branches of the Enoch Pratt Free Library, which are the two proposed sites for program funding from the Annie E. Casey Foundation, are focal points of both neighborhoods where they are located. Community groups use the branches

---

Grant Proposal — *Continued*

---

to hold meetings or social activities. The Pennsylvania Branch has been an anchor for the "revitalization of The Avenue," and Brooklyn has strong and innovative youth programming which has been coordinated with the local schools.

Organizational Structure
Generally regarded as one of the outstanding free libraries in the United States, the Enoch Pratt Free Library was created by Maryland Law in 1882, which enabled the City to accept the donation from Enoch Pratt to establish "The Enoch Pratt Free Library of Baltimore City." The Library is owned by the City but is administered by a private Board of Directors, many of whom are residents of the City of Baltimore or surrounding counties. State Law designates the Enoch Pratt Central Library as a State Library Resource Center. Thus, the Central Library serves all of Maryland through an information sharing system.

The City's library system consists of the Central Library as well as the extensive branch system. The branch system's circulation is 1.0 million per year with approximately 338,100 reference and 147,500 phone questions answered. Annual attendance is estimated at 139,400. The Central Library's circulation is 352,000 per year with approximately 158,700 reference and 201,900 phone questions answered. Annual attendance is estimated at 423,400 patrons per year.

The City's branch system consists of four library districts. Each district has a branch that serves as a District Headquarters for in-depth services such as an extensive reference and periodical collection, online reference services, and microcomputers. Community libraries are located within each district. The community libraries provide basic library services and are designed to serve the information needs of elementary, middle and high school children.

The Enoch Pratt Free Library Budget includes the following funding sources: city support; state per capita; fines/fees; income (Pratt's gift to the City); state and federal funds and special funds totaling $21,605,847 for FY 1997. In addition to the these funds, the Library also receives gifts, income from its endowment and other grants. In FY 1997, the Library expects to receive approximately $1.5 million from these sources. These funds are used to support costs which are not supported by the basic library budget such as, Training, Marketing, and Development. In addition, these funds are used

Grant Proposal — *Continued*

to match or supplement items such as, the funding of special programs, books/materials and technology enhancements.

Proposed Program
Overview of Program
The Enoch Pratt Free Library has a long tradition of providing innovative services for children and youth in Baltimore and has been acknowledged as a national leader in recognizing the importance of working with young people. As part of its mission to create new educational opportunities, a new Pratt pilot project, designed to open the information superhighway to children who might otherwise be denied access, was launched by Mayor Kurt Schmoke on April 28, 1995. The project, titled, A Whole New World: Electronic Information Literacy (*A Whole New World*), is currently being conducted at four Pratt Branches. Broadway, Hollins-Payson, Walbrook and the State Library Resource Center/Central Library, two of which are located within Baltimore's Empowerment Zone. With assistance from The Annie E. Casey Foundation for start-up funding, it is the goal of the Enoch Pratt Library to extend the project into additional branches and create opportunities for more at-risk children.

Statement of Need
The project, *A Whole New World,* was prompted in part by 1994 data, which confirmed what most people already suspected and other studies have found: socio-economic status has a direct impact on who uses computers and how they are used; the electronic information highway is closed, both at home and school, to many poor children. The primary objective of A *Whole New World* was to target a group of these children and, through careful training, guide them on the information superhighway in ways that will motivate them to continue their journey. In addition, A *Whole New World* responds to a recent survey conducted by the Pratt Library which reveals that children under the age of 12 comprise approximately 38.1% of customers using the Library. It also indicates that the most important reason why 82.3% of the surveyed customers come to the Library is for educational support or to do homework.

The plan to extend A *Whole New World* to additional branches is a result of the pilot's success and the need for more children to have access to computer technology. To date, 97 children have com-

Grant Proposal — *Continued*

pleted their Internet training and many are returning to the Library for ongoing use of the program and other available educational computer services.

Characteristics of Community Served
In the first phase of extension, three branches have been identified as having the greatest need for free access to computer training: Pimlico, Pennsylvania, and Brooklyn. Similar to the branches included in the pilot, these three additional branches are located in depressed areas where the majority of the youth population have little or no opportunity for computer education access and could benefit from the electronic literacy goals of the *Whole New World* project.

Desired Outcomes and Evaluation of Outcomes
The desired outcomes for A *Whole New World* include the following:
• to reach, train, and motivate a minimum of 100 new children-at-risk through the *Whole New World Program* in 1997 and to achieve a 90% course-completion rate with this new group
• to help these children develop basic computer literacy skills
• to train these children on the Internet and improve their knowledge of other forms of electronic information
• to train these children to become trainers and mentors for others
   Outcomes will be measured through the use of a pre-test and post-test process. Volunteers will administer a pre-test to determine the trainee's prior use of the Library, computer knowledge, and level of skills. Post-tests will then be completed by the student after the training period to help evaluate the success of the training.

Program Activities
A *Whole New World* trains nine to fourteen year-olds to gain access to information through the Internet, communicate with children world-wide, and use educational databases with pertinent magazine and newspaper articles. As a computer-based program, A *Whole New World* was designed to engage students more effectively than when using traditional methods of teaching through books and classroom instruction. This innovative medium grabs the child's immediate attention through stimulating visuals, sound, and interactive

Grant Proposal — *Continued*

programming. The program also provides an effective vehicle for students to improve their basic literacy skills, while also teaching them how to communicate more effectively through correspondence programs.

A *Whole New World* includes its own packet of motivational materials: an introductory booklet, a student driver's license for the information highway, a study handbook, pencils and keychains with the project motif, certificates for those who complete the training course, and, most importantly, computers for the exclusive use of students enrolled in the program.

Student "drivers" begin by learning basic information about the computer and how it works. A typing tutorial, "Mavis Beacon Teaches Typing," is also available if children need keyboard training. These drivers learn that the Internet is a group of thousands of individual computer networks that allow traffic to pass among them. It is during this first session that all students receive an e-mail account and address and choose a password. The students are then trained in the following areas: E-Mail, where students learn about electronic mail and netiquette and they practice their skills by sending messages to President Clinton, Baltimore Mayor Kurt Schmoke, and fellow *Whole New World* participants; Online Chat, where they speak with other children; "Sailor," the state's computer library network, which gives students access to online catalogs, public information sources, and the Internet; Veronica, an application that searches gopherspace by keyword to look for resources in various subject areas that interest students most; FTP (file transfer protocol) where student drivers go to remote sites and download a copy of Dr. Martin Luther King, Jr.'s "I Have a Dream" speech "the Legend of Sleepy Hollow," or other fun things on the Internet; Telnet, where students use remote logins to play a game of chess or read an article from *USA Today* and finally The Web. The Web sessions allow students to browse World Wide Web resources with Lynx (a text-only browser) and Netscape (with sound and graphics). They also access a list of 10 interesting web sites to explore using their new skills.

This test drive of the Internet helps children understand how to use the technology for information and recreation. They also learn what an integral role the Library plays in bringing the technology to them.

Grant Proposal — *Continued*

Community Involvement

Providing the student with one-on-one intensive training was a primary objective of the *Whole New World* project. The planning and implementation included volunteers from the community along with parents, teachers, and principals who provided additional support. The Program is now staffed by trained volunteers and professional librarians and continues to involve the children's parents as well. All of this has been a key factor in creating a meaningful experience for the student. Scooter, the program's mascot, helps volunteer tutors guide children through the workbook with eight one-hour or two-hour skill building sessions over an eight-week period. Volunteer-student teams are given a deadline for finishing the lessons. For many volunteers, this was their first opportunity to work with at-risk children and their commitment to the project has proved invaluable. In many cases, community volunteers have served as mentors building relationships with students that have continued beyond the training period.

Long-Term Funding

Stating "Youth Services and Education Support" as its number one initiative in its three-year Strategic Plan, the Enoch Pratt Library has already begun to expand the level of library service to children and youth through the *Whole New World* initiative and other important services. As top priorities, these youth initiatives will be incorporated into the Library's future operating budget. Other initiatives include but are not limited to: more intensive orientation materials and on-the-job training for Children's and Young Adult librarians; implementing a plan for parental involvement for all libraries; strengthening, and formalizing ongoing homework support groups; establishing working contacts in each public, private, and parochial school within the city boundaries; establishing coordinated outreach services to preschool educators and parents; increasing holdings of materials in multimedia formats for children and youth.

Whole New World
Budget Narrative

Overall Budget
The $57,000 budget for the *Whole New World* project is composed of $34,000 in one-time-only funds and $23,000 in ongoing costs. Requested funds ($20,000) from the Annie E. Casey Foundation will be matched by $37,000 from public and private sources resulting in a 65% match. Both public and private sources of funds have been secured. Approximately 95% of the budgeted funds will be used to provide direct services to disadvantaged children and families.

One-time-only Funds
Funds from the Annie E. Casey Foundation would support approximately 59% of the one-time-only costs. One-time-only costs include the purchase of computer equipment, furniture, and software to support six (6) public workstations in the three (3) targeted branch sites.

Ongoing Costs
Ongoing costs will be supported through the Library's regular operating budget and include salary, telecommunication, equipment maintenance, utility, training, and the purchase of materials directly related to delivery of service. Overhead costs, which represent less than 5% of the total budget, are for project oversight.

Grant Proposal — *Continued*

Whole New World
Project Budget
(First Phase Extension)

Start-up Costs (one time only)	Casey Request	Trustee Funds	Public Funds	Total Budget
Equipment:				
6 Computers/Printers	11,040	5,520		16,560
Network Connection, etc.	6,140	3,070		9,210
Computer Workstations/Chairs			4,000	4,000
Software	2,820	1,410		4.230
	20,000	10,000	4,000	34,000
Ongoing Costs				
Project Management Salaries*				
5% Youth Services Coordinator			2,500	2,500
Branch Salaries				
5% Branch Manager Salaries			7,500	7,500
5% Children's Librarian Salaries			4,500	4,500
Software/Supplies/Brochures		500	3,500	4,000
Telecommunications/Utilities			2,000	2,000
Training		500		500
Equipment Maintenance/Repairs			2,000	2,000
	0	1,000	22,000	23,000
TOTAL	20,000	11,000	26,000	57,000

*Denotes administrative/overhead cost

Grant Proposal — *Continued*

ENOCH PRATT FREE LIBRARY

(To be administered by volunteer)

WHOLE NEW WORLD "PRE-TEST"

Participant's name _____

Tutor's name _____

Library _____

Date _____

1. What school do you attend?
2. What grade are you in?
3. What Pratt Library branch have used before?
4. Do you have a library card?
5. Had you heard about the Internet before this program?
6. Have you used the computer before?
7. If yes, can you tell me how you use it?
8. Can you type or use a computer keyboard?
9. Do you know what the following things are?

   Telnet
   "Sailor"
   E-mail
   Archie
   Veronica

Our main goal is to educate, our main tactic is to keep it fun!

Grant Proposal — *Continued*

ENOCH PRATT FREE LIBRARY

(To be administered by volunteer)

WHOLE NEW WORLD "PRE-TEST"

Participant's name _____

Tutor's name _____

Library _____

Date _____

  1. What is your e-mail address?

  2. Name the parts of the computer?

  3. What is your favorite WEB SITE?

  4. Who have you communicated with in another country?

  5. Name one library database that you used during training?

  6. Can you download one e-mail message you received and one you sent?

  7. What did you like best about this project?

  8. Was there anything that you did not like?

  9. What changes would you make?

10. Would tell your friends about the project?

11. Do you want your friends to learn what you know?

REFERENCES

1. Carol M. Kurzig, *Foundation Fundamentals: A Guide for Grant Seekers* (New York, Foundation Center, 1981).
2. Paul H. Schneiter, *The Art of Asking: How to Solicit Philanthropic Gifts.* 2d ed. (Rockville, MD: Fundraising Institute, 1985), 5.
3. Victoria Steele and Stephen D. Elder, *Becoming a Fundraiser: The Principles and Practice of Library Development* (Chicago: American Library Association, 1992), 104.
4. Steele and Elder, 105.
5. Steele and Elder, 107.
6. Kurzig, 12.
7. Ernest Imhoff, "Foundation Aims to Bring Commitment to Action Here," *The Sun*, (17 Jan. 1996), 3B.

Chapter 7

Beyond the Bay: Model Programs Elsewhere

*From a personal perspective, I think that libraries play a very
critical role in providing a point of entry for youth at-risk. . . .
They [libraries] constitute a much better return on investment
because you can permanently put something out there for young
people that none of them feel intimidated about regardless of
whether or not they have "Air Jordan" [sport shoes], and the
appropriate athletic ability. They can all compete on a fair playing
field in the confines of the library.*
—Floyd Johnson, city manager, Fort Lauderdale, Fla.

Historically, public libraries have served countless teens at risk creatively and effectively. The BALIS project represents by far the most comprehensive and ambitious model. The innovative mix of initiatives (youth summits, task forces, focus groups, special programs, etc.) in the BALIS project offers librarians who desire to implement at-risk programs a variety of techniques and programming ideas. Other public libraries nationwide have also developed similar innovative and effective ways to serve at-risk youth in their communities. These notable programs ranging from late night storytelling for incarcerated teens to Internet literacy training demonstrate that libraries continue to make a difference in the lives of thousands of young people who need them.

You can customize the featured techniques, programs, and services in this chapter to suit the needs of the young people in your community.

YOUTH SUMMIT

Targeted "traditional" library services to the disadvantaged were addressed in earnest at the Enoch Pratt Free Library in Baltimore, Maryland, in 1967. At that time, Lowell Martin, recognized in his study
Baltimore Reaches Out: Library Service to the Disadvantaged[1] that a segment of the city's population needed special attention from the library.
By today's standards that population would be considered at-risk because
of their economic status, lack of education, and poor living conditions.
The document enabled the library to enhance and improve many of its
services to assist this targeted audience. In 1993, 26 years later, Pratt
Library continued in that tradition by holding a daylong summit, "What's
Urban Got to Do With It?: Library Services to Children and Youth." The
summit sought to:

- address any barriers that might be unique to the urban environment and that could possibly prevent the effective delivery of library services.
- look for opportunities that might be unique to the urban environment and that could enhance the delivery of library services.
- find examples of exemplary programs supporting children and
  youth in an urban setting.

At the summit, staff addressed the numerous challenges and opportunities facing the library in an urban setting, where many young people
were at-risk. Several ideas that grew out of the summit led to greater
service enhancements for young people. The morning's opening session
included a keynote speaker who worked with young at-risk African-
American males and a candid teenage panel that discussed library-related issues and concerns. The panel of teens had already prepared their
responses to the question: "If you were in charge of the library what
would change and why?" Many on the panel indicated that library hours
needed changing. They also thought that there needed to be greater opportunities for teen involvement in library activities along with better
communication between the library and the public school system.

During the afternoon session, staff divided into small groups to discuss four topics: services to schools, collection development, summer
reading, and training. Based on the small group discussions, the planning committee developed a select list of ideas, suggestions, and recommendations that was given further consideration by several project
teams of youth services librarians.

Planning a Summit

Planning a summit is similar to planning any other program:

- Create a planning committee of three to five people.
- Develop the committee's charge (e.g., to make plans to review, revitalize, or enhance current services for at-risk youth).
- Determine the objectives (e.g., to develop creative ways to deliver services to young people).
- Develop and categorize critical areas you need to address in your service delivery (e.g., funding, staff training, policies and procedures, programming, and collection development). It is best to finalize the categories after polling all youth services librarians about what they see as challenges, barriers, and opportunities to providing programs and services for this audience.
- Determine the format (e.g., keynote speaker, breakout sessions, reporting back period for the day, and follow-up process).
- Develop an agenda for the summit (see Figure 7.1).
- Determine who should attend (e.g., all youth services librarians, library director, teens, and librarians from other libraries, and community youth services providers).
- Develop a list of potential keynote speakers. If possible, choose a youth-oriented, knowledgeable, and inspirational one. Invite the person to speak for approximately 30 minutes and have a 10- to 15-minute question-and-answer period.
- Select several possible days and dates. No date is ideal; however, the final selection involves negotiating the schedules of many of the attendees (e.g., the library director, staff, keynote speaker, and teens).
- Choose a convenient location to convene the summit.
- Develop a budget for refreshments and incidentals.
- Identify potential staff to serve as facilitators for breakout sessions.
- Meet with session's facilitators to discuss summit's objectives, their roles, room and topic assignments, and needed supplies.
- Develop a resource list of relevant articles and reports to send to all participating staff for review prior to the summit (e.g., teen demographics, school performance, teen library use, instances of successful library intervention, etc.).
- Decide which staff will attend each breakout session, and develop pertinent information related to the discussion topics. Send this information as is appropriate to each breakout session participant.

Figure 7.1
Sample Youth Summit Agenda Enoch Pratt Free Library Youth Summit "What's Urban Got to Do with It?" October 22, 1993 AGENDA

9:00 a.m. – 9:30 a.m.
Central Library
POE ROOM
COFFEE

MORNING PROGRAM—WHEELER AUDITORIUM

9:30 a.m. – 9:45 a.m.
REMARKS, DR. CARLA HAYDEN, DIRECTOR
REMARKS, SARA SIEBERT, RETIRED
YOUNG ADULT SERVICES COORDINATOR

9:45 a.m. – 10:00 a.m.
STATE OF YOUTH SERVICES
DEBORAH TAYLOR, OFFICE OF CHILDREN AND YOUTH

10:00 a.m. – 11:15 a.m.
KEYNOTE SPEECH
KEVIN MERCER, PROJECT SITE COORDINATOR
CENTER FOR EDUCATING THE AFRICAN-AMERICAN MALE

11:15 a.m. – 11:30 a.m.
BREAK

11:30 a.m. – 12:15 p.m.
YOUTH PANEL
EUNICE HARPER, MODERATOR

12:15 p.m. – 1:15 p.m.
LUNCH—STAFF LOUNGE

1:30 p.m. – 3:00 p.m.
BREAKOUT SESSIONS

3:00 p.m. – 3:15 p.m.
BREAK

3:15 p.m. – 4:30 P.M.
REPORTS FROM BREAKOUT SESSIONS
POE ROOM

4:30 p.m. – 4:45 p.m.
"WHERE DO WE GO FROM HERE?"
DR. HAYDEN

Figure 7.2			
Youth Summit To-Do List			
To Do	**Status**	**Responsible**	**Comment**
Articles for breakout sessions		AT	Have been identified
Facilitator's meeting	8 a.m. 10/19	KL	Agenda completed
Walk-thru	9 a.m. 10/6	KL, PM, AT	Check staff lounge
Youth panel		LH, AT	Complete questions
Guest speakers	follow-up 10/5	PM	Confirmed
Room signs	Request sent to PR	AT	
Facilitators		AT	Get flip chart, pens, etc.
Lunch	menu developed	KL	Box lunches/beverages
Name tags	purchase tags	AT	Markers needed
Facilities staff contact		AT	
Coffee		AT	Lounge/Blue Room
Hosts for invited guest	Greeters selected	KL	
Required memos		KL, PM, AT	
Budget	In process	PM	Requires approval
Press coverage/photos		PR, RP	Confirmed
Thank-you (follow-up)		PM	
Follow-up plan		KL, PM, AT	
Invitations for guests	Mail by 10/6	AT	revise draft
Program	Print by 10/18	PR	developed

- To keep committee members on task develop a detailed to-do list. (see Figure 7.2).

TASK FORCE MODEL

Strategic long-range plans for a three-to-five year period for the library in general may allow you the opportunity to place youth services in the context of a bigger picture. In this case, the library director may appoint a task force for purposes of developing or revitalizing services specifically for at-risk teens. About eight team members could take up to six months to gather and analyze data similar to that of the needs assessment detailed in Chapter Four. Specifically, those areas should include demographics; current service, if any; the impact of the external environment on teens; changes in technology; and best practices, model programs, and services elsewhere. Additionally, a review is also needed of prospective and current community partners, related services to youth by other agencies, the impact of library policies and procedures, and the relevance of the project to broader community concerns and priorities.

Task Force Assignment

- Collect and analyze important data in the external environment (see Figure 7.3).
- Determine how the information affects the lives of at-risk teens. For example, gathering information about teens' access to technology, their job responsibilities, reading and math scores, and demographics may help in deciding where and how the library can better serve them.
- Assess the library's capacity to deliver a new or expanded service.
- Collect and analyze data in the internal environment as it relates to teens. Include the number and types of programs, size of staff, funding levels, and library policies and procedures. If possible, compare the data to similar information from nearby libraries or other services within the library.
- Develop ideas and set goals and objectives. Keep your recommendations within the context of the data analysis and assumptions. For example, a good recommendation might read: "The task force recommends that the library provide Internet training." This recommendation was based on family poverty levels and the limited access of teens to computers, along with their inability to find and adequately use information from the Internet for homework assignments and for pleasure.

Figure 7.3

The Community Free Library Assessment

COMMUNITY FREE LIBRARY ASSESSMENT

Population:
Total 30,634
54% African American, 44% White
54% of population 19 years and under
6,966 families live in the library's service area
41% of all families are headed by females

Income and Employment:
Median Income - $15,910
33% of all families live below the poverty level
Unemployment rate 18% males – 16% females
5,688 households receive public assistance

Health:
A study of physician supply and demand revealed that community is medically underserved as defined by federal guidelines. The rate of births and abortions in this area is higher than the City's median. Adolescent births and abortions for females ages 12-17 for 2,000 was 1,836 births; 69 induced abortions.

Education:
Of the 7,847 persons 25 years and older with some formal education, 2,072 are high school graduates; 1,156 have completed 1-4 years or more of college. Total persons enrolled in school ages three and over, are 8,116. Of that, 253 are in nursery school; 5,148 are in elementary school; 1,190 are in high school; and 726 are in college.

Library Use:
Approximately 90% of the users are African American and between the ages of 5 to 25. Approximately 80% of the library users request informational and educational related materials.

Figure 7.3 — *Continued*

Library Use (continued):
Library users require information on a basic level in many subject areas, particularly drugs, health, jobs, sex, and criminal law. The library is the major resource for information in the community. However, community members seeking specific information on health care, public assistance, housing, employment, and education have the following resources available:

- Bon Secours Hospital Information Center
- C.O.O.L. (Community Organized for the Improvement of Life)
- Department of Social Services
- The External High School
- University of Maryland Hospital Information Center
- Urban Services
- West Baltimore Community Health Care Center

Priority Print and Nonprint Materials for Young Adults:

- Sports
- Abortion
- Sex
- Pregnancy
- Black interest (fiction and nonfiction)
- Romance

- Draft a list of potential community partners who will support the recommended initiatives (see figure 7.4).

"I DREAM A DREAM" FOCUS GROUP

What would you do for at-risk teens if you had more than enough money and staff? This is a question designed to encourage creative thinking with no-holds-barred brainstorming and no need for reality checks. The technique can yield many innovative special project ideas worthy of development for grant funding. Sometimes, with modifications, you can implement one of the ideas with library funding. While the session may last for only one day, a good deal of preliminary preparation is required.

Figure 7.4

Community Partners List

Advocates for Children and Youth
300 Cathedral Street Suite 300
Baltimore, Maryland 21201
410-542-9200

Archdioceses of Baltimore
Office of Family Life
320 Cathedral Street
Baltimore, Maryland 21201
410-547-5508

Baltimore Reads Incorporated
330 N. Charles Street
Baltimore, Maryland 21201
410-752-3595

Baltimore Council of
Adolescent Pregnancy . . .
1304 St. Paul Street
Baltimore, Maryland 21202
410-752-2922

Baltimore Urban League, Inc.
1150 Mondawmin Concourse
Baltimore, Maryland 21215
410-523-8150

Big Brother and Big Sister of
Central Maryland, Inc.
2220 St. Paul Street
Baltimore, Maryland 21218
410-243-4000

Children and Youth Program
Francis Scott Key Medical
4940 Eastern Avenue
Baltimore, Maryland 21224
410-550-0100

Collegebound Foundation
204 E. Lombard Street
Baltimore, Maryland 21215
410-783-2905

Echo House Multi Service Center, Inc.
1705 W. Fayette Street
Baltimore, Maryland 21223
410-947-1700

Junior League of Baltimore
4803 Roland Avenue
Baltimore, Maryland 21210
410-467-0260

North Central Youth Services
5501 Ivanhoe Avenue
Baltimore, Maryland 21212
410-323-5020

Northwest Baltimore Youth
3319 W. Belvedere Avenue
Baltimore, Maryland 21215
410-578-8100

Office for Children and Youth
301 W. Preston Street
Baltimore, Maryland 21201
410-225-4160

Salvation Army Boys and Girls
Club of Baltimore
2602 Huntingdon Avenue
Baltimore, Maryland 21211
410-366-4894

Teen Parenting Enrichment Program
1429 McCulloh Street
Baltimore, Maryland 21217
410-728-7878

Youth Diversions Programs
321 Fallsway
Baltimore, Maryland 21202
410-333-6841

To effectively generate ideas, select inspiring, thought provoking material for the participants to read prior to the meeting.

The Process

- Decide on the steps you will take for further review and development of ideas. Will a youth advisory group react and refine the ideas? Will a library project team implement the developed ideas?
- Select up to six creative thinkers. Include library staff as well as community-based providers.
- To set the tone, establish ground rules, and use a facilitator familiar with focus group dynamics and brainstorming techniques to record ideas.
- Before they attend the session, ask the participants to think about how the library presently relates to youth, including the condition and physical layout of the building, available print and nonprint material; services and programs, and hours of service.
- Vote, and then prioritize the group's ideas based upon the idea receiving the most votes to the one that gets the least votes.

SPECIAL PROGRAMS OR PROJECTS

Young people enjoy programs in which they can interact with and learn from a responsible adult. The projects described in this section fit one of the six categories indicated by Harde and Kibbe's[2] evaluation of the BALIS project initiative. These are providing information about services, young adult collection and facility development, programs for youth, tutoring programs, community outreach, and integrating youth into the library. These programs also have the proven ingredients necessary for success with young people—individual attention, a welcoming/caring environment, peer involvement, and social and life skills training.

Excellence in Library Services to Young Adults

Excellence in Library Services to Young Adults[3] features several programs tailored for at-risk teens including those that are easily adaptable. The programs designated with an asterisk (*) are not spefically identified as programs for at-risk teens, but are suitable.

CHICAGO PUBLIC LIBRARY—MALE MENTORING/READ ALOUD PROGRAM (RAP)

What: A male mentoring read-aloud program offered in a poor, high crime, low-income, African American neighborhood. This collaborative project involved the library, a high school, and the children's museum. Fifteen high school mentors, trained in storytelling and homework assistance, work one-on-one with younger males.

Contact: Hall Branch Library, 4801 S. Michigan Ave., Chicago, IL 60615, (312) 747-2541.

DEKALB COUNTY (GA.) PUBLIC LIBRARY—BUILDING BLOCKS TO LITERACY: A LITERACY PROGRAM FOR TEEN PARENTS AND THEIR INFANTS

What: A program that targets teen parents between 15 and 18. The program enables young parents to become their child's first teacher by helping them to involve their children in activities that lead to development of language skills. In six-week sessions librarians instruct parents on ways to share books, rhymes, puppets, and stories with their children. As a result of the program, the parents report that they read, sing, and play regularly with their infants.

Contact: Dekalb County Public Library, 215 Sycamore St., Decatur, GA 30030, (404) 370-8458.

DETROIT (MICH.) PUBLIC LIBRARY—AUTHOR DAY*

What: A reading incentive program. Author Day originated in "one of the most socially, economically and educationally depressed areas of Detroit"[3] and expanded to include several library branches as well as the main library. For students in grades seven through nine, the program served as an incentive to read for recreational purposes. The students read a minimum of three books from a list of young adult titles and in school they discuss the books and authors on the list. After the discussions, they complete "Author Day" book report forms and vote for a favorite author. The winning author is invited to speak at a luncheon attended by several of the students.

Contact: Hubbard Branch Library, Detroit Public Library, 12929 W. McNichols, Detroit, MI 48235, (313) 935-3434.

MONROE COUNTY PUBLIC LIBRARY (BLOOMINGTON, IND.)—YOUNG ADULT BOOK SELECTION

What: A program designed to encourage recreational reading among at-risk youth. Westside Center Library teens receive snacks, training, and the opportunity to read, review, and purchase books for the young adult collection. The majority of the participants performed poorly in school and did not use the library. The visits to the bookstores to buy books for the young adult collection increased the teens comfort levels with both the library and the bookstore.

Contact: Monroe County Public Library, 303 E. Kirkwood Ave., Bloomington, IN 47408, (812) 339-2271.

SAN DIEGO (CALIF.) PUBLIC LIBRARY—HOMEWORK CENTERS

What: Satellite homework centers in high-risk communities to support the library's outreach efforts. The centers, which are located in library branches, recreation centers, housing complexes, YMCAs, and Boys and Girls Clubs, have basic reference collections and provide volunteer tutoring.

Contact: San Diego Public Library, 820 E. St., San Diego, CA 92101-6778, (619) 236-5830.

CHICAGO PUBLIC LIBRARY—LIBRARY BASEBALL TEAM

What: A library sponsored baseball team comprised mostly of Arab, Hispanic and African Americans, and Eastern Europeans. This collaborative outreach effort reaches out to underserved youngsters and allows the library to contribute to this multicultural community, as well as improve its image. At the end of the season participants receive books and trophies, compliments of the library.

Contact: West Lawn Library, 4020 W. 63 St., Chicago, IL 60629, (312) 747-7381.

CHICAGO PUBLIC LIBRARY—HALL AND ROBERT TAYLOR HOMES JOB TRAINING

What: Eight-week job training sessions. In these sessions teens learn about resume writing, interviewing, dressing for success, appropriate work behaviors, and the application process. Participants also worked eight hours a week in the library and visited several workplaces. Upon completion of the program, the library holds a graduation ceremony and the teens receive a $300 stipend. Many of the teens have become regular library users.

Contact: Hall Branch Library, 4801 Michigan Ave., Chicago, IL 60615, (312) 747-2541.

District of Columbia Public Library and the School without Walls Youth Exchange—(Washington, D.C.) School and Library Reading Program

What: A cooperative effort between the library and a local school, to encourage reading and lifelong library users among the city's high school at-risk students. Teens read one book a week, participate in book discussions at the library, prepare and present booktalks, and receive "service learning" credits.

Contact: District of Columbia Public Library, 901 G. St., NW Room 109, Washington, DC 20001, (202) 727-1295.

Iberia Parish Library—(New Iberia, La.)—Passport to Excitement and Adventure: Summer Workshops*

What: Creative workshops with appeal to youngsters aged 12–17. The workshops cover a variety of subjects—model rocketry, bread making, camping, fitness, and natural science. Each participant attends two workshops and receives both a practical and educational approach to learning about a specific topic. Staff noted that the bookmark bibliographies received at the end of the sessions helped to increase circulation. The project is highly rated by its participants and greatly supported by parents, business owners, workshop leaders, and the media.

Contact: Iberia Parish Library, 445 E. Main St., New Iberia, LA 70560, (318) 373-0075.

Meriden Public Library—(Meriden, Ct.)—Summer-on-Site Computer Camp

What: A summer computer camp for at-risk young adults between the ages of 14 and 21. The library used a state block grant to establish the camp. Participants learned computer skills and job preparation techniques. In addition to attending classes in the library, the young adults worked in several other city departments.

Contact: Meriden Public Library, Meriden, CT 06450, (203) 238-2344, ext.14.

Riverside (Calif.) City and County Public Library, Riverside Unified School District, and Alvord Unified School District—Homework Assistance, Youth Advocacy Council, Library Representation on Citywide Committees

What: Programs developed in response to the Los Angeles riots that support at-risk youth. Several community organizations in Riverside joined

together to develop a host of programs. They opened several homework assistance centers for middle school students. The Youth Advocacy Council planned programs and made suggestions for video and book selections. The youth service librarians increased their visibility and influence by serving on several citywide youth-serving committees.
Contact: Riverside City and County Public Library, 3021 Franklin St., Riverside, CA 92507, (909) 369-3003.

Austin (Tex.) Public Library—VICTORY (Volunteers in Communities Tutoring Our Responsible Youth)

What: A one-to-one volunteer homework assistance program.
Contact: Austin Public Library, P.O. Box 2287, Austin, TX 78766, (512) 499-7325.

King County Library System—(Seattle, Wa.)—Library in Juvenile Detention

What: The library located in the juvenile detention center to support the informational, recreational, and educational needs of incarcerated youth. Librarians provide access to the well-used print and nonprint materials. Youth have access to an extensive collection that includes books, music, magazines, posters, cassettes, comics, newspapers, puzzles, and pamphlets. Library staff members also engage the youth in creative reading and writing activities. One objective of this program is to encourage young people to see the library as a resource beyond incarceration.
Contact: King County Public Library, 1211 E. Adler, Seattle, WA 98212, (206) 343-2641.

Cuyahoga County Public Library—(Cleveland, Ohio)— Leap Ahead

What: Kits on loan for "informationally disadvantaged" young adults in hospitals, homeless shelters, and rehabilitation clinics. The 50 subject-related kits contain books, audio- and videocassettes, posters, games, activity ideas, pamphlets, and booklists. Topics covered include AIDS, conflict resolution, parenting, self-esteem, and teen issues.
Contact: Mayfield Regional Branch, Cuyahoga County Public Library, 6080 Wilson Mills Rd., Cleveland, OH 44143, (216) 473-0350.

MIAMI-DADE (FLA.) PUBLIC LIBRARY SYSTEM—ANNUAL BLACK HISTORY MONTH OUTREACH

What: Symposium targeted for African-American youth during Black History Month featuring community leaders. At the symposium, successful black role models share their experiences. Among the speakers are judges, police officers, doctors, lawyers, and religious leaders. The leaders challenge the young people to look beyond negative images and envision the possibilities before them.

Contact: North Dade Regional Library, 2455 NW 1183 St., Miami, FL 33056, (305) 625-6424.

WYMORE CAREER EDUCATION CENTER, ORANGE COUNTY SCHOOLS— (EATONVILLE, FLA.)—BREAKING THE CYCLE

What: Teen parents, grades 7–12, learn about children's literature and the importance of reading to their children. Teens develop ways to share books with their children by using finger plays, nursery rhymes, and fairy tales, and they create books for their children. Visits to the library allow the youth to check out books related to the project.

Contact: Wymore Career Education Center, 100 E. Kennedy Blvd., Eatonville, FL 32751, (407) 644-7518, ext. 208.

EMPORIA (KANS.) PUBLIC LIBRARY—RITES OF PASSAGE

What: Discussion groups for African-American males. On several summer afternoons, 25 young African-American males met for three hours at the public library to discuss topics related to growing into adulthood. Emporia Public Library and Emporia State University developed the reality-based discussion sessions to enable the young men to better evaluate and plan their lives. Discussion topics included self-esteem, peer pressure, racism, role models, self-determination, sexual relationships, male and female roles, employment opportunities, racism in employment, social outlets and conditions, goal setting, and post-secondary educational opportunities. At the end of program, each young man received a certificate.

Contact: Emporia Public Library, 110 E. Sixth Ave., Emporia, KS 66801, (316) 342-6524.

NEW YORK (N.Y.) PUBLIC LIBRARY—YOUNG ADULT MURAL PROJECT

What: A young adult painting project easily adapted to an at-risk audience. During the summer at the Chatham Square Branch Library of the New York Public Library, about 20 youngsters, assisted by an artist, planned, designed, and created a permanent painting for the library. The youth in this Chinatown community created a beautiful mural they called Community in Motion. The time spent by the youngsters in making this visible contribution enhanced their team-building and planning skills, and the project increased the bond between the library and the community at-large.

Contact: Chatham Square Regional Branch, New York Public Library, 33 E. Broadway, New York, NY 10002, (212) 964-6598.

More Models and Ideas

For the most part, the programs in this section are easy to replicate, inexpensive, and have minor staffing implications.

T.A.P. (TEEN AGENCY PROGRAM)

This is an outreach program at Allen County Public Library in Fort Wayne, Indiana, that serves teens in several institutions. Librarians develop and maintain deposit collections at juvenile hall, juvenile correctional facilities, a shelter for neglected and abused children, a residential school for emotional disturbed youth, and a drop-in teen center. They replenish the collections monthly. Booktalking and summer reading programs take place in each participating agency. During "The Late Show," just after lights out, trained adult volunteers provide nighttime comfort to institutionalized teens by reading stories, playing music, and talking. This award winning, innovative program allows adults to calm and comfort teens so they can sleep better at night. "The Late Show" has sparked many teens' interest in reading and listening to the written word. A volunteer at the Contra Costa County Juvenile Hall in Martinez, California, created the program with assistance from the library staff.

Contact: Allen County Public Library, 900 Webster St., Fort Wayne, IN 46801, (219) 424-7241.

GREAT TRANSITIONS (STRUGGLE, CHANGE, ACHIEVE)

This is a program that provides library services to incarcerated juveniles as well as to those out on probation. In 1997, the Hennepin County and Minneapolis Public Libraries and Hennepin County Home School collaborated with several community agencies to implement Great Transitions. Figure 7.5 is a collaboration chart from the program. With this program, institutionalized teens are able to take advantage of and benefit from the services provided by the library. The project began with five clear goals:

Figure 7.5			
Collaboration Chart			
TYPE OF ORGANIZATION COLLABORATIVE	**NAME OF ORGANIZATION OR COLLABORATIVE**	**SERVICE THAT ORGANIZATIONS WILL OFFER NUMBER**	**KEY CONTACT PERSON AND PHONE**
Juvenile detention facility	Hennepin County Home School	Staff time & services	Terry Wise, Superintendent 949-4521
Public School	EPSILON program, Hopkins School District	Staff time direct service to students in classroom consultation with library staff	Char Myklebust, Coordinator 949-4570
Juvenile Corrections	Hennepin County Juvenile Probation	Staff time & services encourage participation at individual release staffing enforce participation in program	Denzil Lue, Correctional Unit Supervisor 949-4600 Fred Brian, Extended Juvenile Jurisdiction Supervisor 348-9720
Public Library	Minneapolis Public Library	Staff time direct services to students at CHS & on site at branch libraries	Adela Peskorz, Coordinator of Young Adult Services, MPL 327-6561
Public Library	Hennepin County Library	Staff time direct services to students at CHS & on site at agencies project leadership & coordination select & process library materials which support programs develop & publish promotional brochures, handouts, etc.	Ali Turner, Project Manager 551-6005 Liz Anderson, HCL Outreach 541-8543

Figure 7.5 — *Continued*

TYPE OF ORGANIZATION COLLABORATIVE	NAME OF ORGANIZATION OR COLLABORATIVE	SERVICE THAT ORGANIZATIONS WILL OFFER NUMBER	KEY CONTACT PERSON AND PHONE
Juvenile Probation	Community Alternative Probation Supervision (CAP), Hennepin County Juvenile Probation	Consultation on program design & implementation	Jack Hower, CAPS Supervisor 348-5391
Volunteers	Parents of current and former CHS residents	Participation in program development & evaluation	to be determined
Volunteers	Current and former CHS students	Participation in program development & evaluation	to be determined

1. To introduce the public library as a vital and engaging setting that addresses relevant concerns and interests of youth in transition.
2. To reach out to teens at a crucial stage in terms of self-identity and personal decision making.
3. To work in partnership with corrections and Epsilon school staffs to further develop students' communication skills.
4. To position library staff and services as viable partners in juvenile aftercare.
5. To educate corrections staff about the ongoing value and services of the library.

The evaluation process includes tracking statistics on new library cards issued and collecting of comments through interviews with corrections staff and teens.

Currently, at the suggestion of the teens, the library is planning to publish their writing and artwork.

Contact: Ali Turner, Great Transitions Project Manager, Hennepin County Library, 15700 36 Ave. N., Plymouth, MN 55446-3263, (612) 551-6005.

> "Thank you for the books you gave us and also the pizza party for lunch. I really appreciate the fact that you asked us to read the books and to make the decisions to what would go on the list. . . . To know I was a factor in creating a list for others to read felt good."
> —Albert, Great Transitions Project

Reaching out to juvenile detention centers offers the library the chance to serve young people who probably have had little exposure to its resources. Additionally, you can maintain a library presence by housing deposit collections of interest at day camps, recreation centers, and halfway houses.

SUMMER READING CAMP, GENEVA FREE LIBRARY IN GENEVA, NEW YORK

For several summers, the library has successfully attracted nonreaders and nonlibrary users to its free one-week basketball and reading camp. Recruitment for participants occurs at schools, free lunch sites, and low income housing programs. Volunteer coaches teach camp attendees basketball fundamentals. The fun-filled noncompetitive reading activities involve the coaches reading aloud, independent reading, word games, trivia hunts, library exploration, and the completion of a daily log. The library receives great publicity for providing a positive reading experience. A series of grants supports the project.
Contact: Geneva Free Library, 244 Main St., Geneva, NY 14456, (315) 789-5303.

"CELEBRATING YOU" YOUTH FAIR AT THE HOWLAND PUBLIC LIBRARY, BEACON, NEW YORK

The "Celebrating You," festival featured a range of multicultural presentations that celebrated the heritages of local teens. Festival attendees learned about Africa, Germany, Ireland, Australia, and Latin America. The library held issues-oriented discussions on topics such as AIDS and violence; served ethnic foods; provided music; and gave away door prizes. Teens received tips on how to write research papers, learned about careers in music, and listened to book talks. After the fair, staff reported a dramatic increase in library use by local area teens. With the formation of a reader's advisory committee, they have helped to expand the young adult collection by adding CDs and multimedia items.

Contact: Howland Public Library, 313 Main St., Beacon, NY 12508, (914) 831-1134.

CLASP (CONNECTING LIBRARIES AND SCHOOLS PROJECT)

CLASP began in 1991 as a three-year pilot project involving 23 branches of the New York Public Library and three school districts. A 3.6 million grant from DeWitt Wallace-Reader's Digest provided the funding. During its pilot phase, the project reached over 120,000 people, including students, parents, and teachers. CLASP's advisory committee members included school and public librarians, parents, teachers, principals, office staff from CLASP and the school districts. This summer reading experience benefited thousands of young people. Coordinated booklists with appropriate titles for summer reading along with substantial numbers of copies of the recommended books enabled young people to locate books easily in the library. Remarkably, the library spent over half of the original funding for materials. Public librarians registered parents and discussed library use with them at parent-teacher conference nights. The success of the three-year pilot lead to the project's expansion to Queens Borough and Brooklyn Public Libraries, as well as to New York City's Board of Education and its local districts. CLASP has three main goals:

1. To support collaboration and cooperation between New York City schools and public libraries.
2. To encourage family reading and family literacy and make it enjoyable.
3. To increase community awareness and use of public libraries.

TEENS CAN'T WAIT! TEEN INITIATIVE, 1997

Teens Can't Wait! was the Atlanta-Fulton County Public Library's all-out effort to attract teens, many of whom were at risk, to special programs throughout their service area. To win over Atlanta's teens, the library implemented an aggressive campaign with an impressive number of teen-related programs, for example, how to write term papers, meet the authors reception, female and male rites of passages, resolving conflicts, surfing the Internet, teen health, resume writing, and career development. In addition, they established a teen advisory board, purchased library materials, and sponsored a teen night to showcase services available to teens throughout the county.

This initiative had seven goals.

1. To develop an aggressive campaign designed to reclaim teenage audiences in libraries.
2. To build partnerships with other youth-serving agencies within the Fulton County service area.
3. To provide materials that support educational goals, career development, and problem-solving skills.
4. To organize a teen advisory board.
5. To create volunteer opportunities for teens in libraries.
6. To sponsor programs and workshops in collaboration with local businesses and other community-based agencies.
7. To conduct seminars and workshops to update skills of staff working with teens.

Several measures were used to evaluate the project's success, including number of teen library cards issued; number of items checked out on teen cards; number of teen programs planned and executed; program attendance; number of school visits to middle and high schools; and quantity of materials purchased for teens. Teens Can't Wait! was made possible with grant funds from the Fulton County Board of Commissioners and generously supported and sponsored by several businesses and community organizations.

Contact: Doris C. Jackson, Atlanta-Fulton Public Library, One Margaret Mitchell Square, Atlanta, GA 30303, (404) 730-1700.

Inexpensive—Quick And Easy

The author created the following inexpensive and moderately easy-to-modify and replicate projects to serve teens at the Hollins-Payson branch of the Enoch Pratt Free Library in Baltimore, Maryland. (See the introduction for details about the Hollins-Payson Library.)

TALENT GALORE

What: A "creative works" bulletin board
Why: To encourage teens to display their talents and enhance their self-esteem.
How: Solicit works of poetry, short stories, essays, and art from teens. Posting a sign is helpful, however one-on-one solicitation is better. Develop formats for display purposes. For example, if your display space is limited, you need to determine a maximum size for contributions. For uniformity, type all of the accepted handwritten works. Take a photograph in the library of each teen whose work is accepted and use the pictures as part of the exhibit. Determine how long to exhibit the mate-

rials. Once the exhibit is over, give the participants copies of their type-written works as well as their library photograph. If you receive a suffi-cient number of poems, essays, and short stories, consider compiling and printing them for distribution to members of the community. Encour-age teens who may not have written before nor had their artwork dis-played to contribute. This project also works well if you want to exhibit works from the community at large.

MATERIALS

- Bulletin board, approximately 6x4 feet
- 35mm camera and film
- Large colorful letters at least nine inches high that spell "TALENT GALORE"
- Poster to solicit entries
- Construction paper in several colors for mounting the poems, es-says, and short stories

TEEN TAX PREPARATION SERVICE

What: Tax preparation classes for teens

Why: Frequently teens are unfamiliar with filing simple tax returns to receive their tax refunds. In many instances, local neighborhood busi-nesses charge excessive fees for tax return preparation and cashing tax refund checks.

How: Offer a tax preparation workshop, develop tips for check cashing, and list the best places in the community for check cashing. A local bank can help with the list. Request a Volunteer Income Tax Assistance per-son (VITA), from the Internal Revenue Service or contact a knowledge-able tax person to conduct the class. Set a time and date for the class during tax season. Send flyers for posting to neighborhood youth ser-vices agencies. Ask teens to contact the library and sign up for the work-shop. The idea of receiving "all my money back" appeals to young people and many of them need check cashing tips. Your role may include in-troducing the instructor, reminding teens to bring their W-2 forms, de-veloping the check cashing tips and location list and, if necessary, supplying the appropriate tax forms.

TRADING PLACES

What: Teens learn about the world of work by focusing on careers in the library.

Why: Many teens do not understand what the library staff does.

How: What follows is an actual report about the program. "Y'all get to sit a lot on this job. All you have to do is answer the phone and show people where the books are. If I were in charge, I would . . . " These were among the many comments made by teens that reflected their views of what it meant to work in a library. A desire to expand their knowledge of library work led to Trading Places. Several young adults experienced the "upstairs/downstairs" activities of a public library. We were pleasantly surprised at their responses. The idea of learning about jobs in the library had great appeal. Within an hour we filled the available positions—branch manager, adult services librarian, children's librarian, desk supervisor, desk assistant, and security guard.

Orientation for each participant included making an appointment with staff to receive a job description and list of duties for their job assignment. Gradually, the staff began to notice that excitement for Trading Places extended to other library users. Many teens expressed disappointment because they were unable to "get a job." Although the teens worked on a day that school was closed, they arrived early, anxious to get started. They spent the morning at the main library. After a warm welcome from the director, the teens proceeded to the human resources office for "first day" orientation. They completed job application forms, picked up their identification badges, and toured the main library. Then it was off to a festive lunch, compliments of the director. In the afternoon, the teen staff worked at a variety of preplanned tasks, which included patron assistance, library card registration, filling out staff schedule sheets, and checking library materials in and out of the library. Several members of the community came to the library just to see the teens at work. When we gathered at the end of the day for one last group photograph with the teens and regular library staff, we sensed that something special had occurred for us all. At any rate, they left proud of their accomplishments, and we did as well.

A FAMILY AFFAIR

What: A Sunday afternoon of fun and entertainment with teens and library staff sharing their many talents with family and friends

Why: We created A Family Affair in an effort to draw families of teen library users to the library and to showcase the teens' talents in the performing arts. The library staff and their families also performed.

How: Planning took nearly three months. We held auditions at the library, and staff and community members selected ten acts. Teens from the community presented seven performances that included original dance interpretations, mime, and singing. Staff family members provided three performances. The entire staff recited a poem as part of their con-

"I can show you the world, shining, shimmering, splendid. I can open your eyes, take you wonder by wonder. A whole new world, a new fantastic point of view. Don't you dare close your eyes. A hundred thousand things to see. A whole new world, with new horizons to pursue. Let me share this whole new world with you."[4]

—Aladdin's Song

"At-risk youth do not view themselves in need of "fixing" or "repair." What they do talk about is the desire for nurturing, respect, and opportunities to develop skills and responsibility."[5]

tribution to the day. Two weeks prior to the event, a large glass showcase caught the attention of many. It contained photographs of the performing teens with their families and library staff with their families. Over two hundred people attended the program. A video preserved this event for posterity, and the day ended with refreshments.

A WHOLE NEW WORLD—TECHNOLOGY

New technology has contributed to widening the gap between the "information rich" and the "information poor." Socio-economic status has had a strong impact on computer use. Experts contend that the computer's capabilities make it especially well suited to the needs of at-risk youth. They are attracted to the multi-sensory method of obtaining information they experience when surfing the Internet. However, providing equity and access are not enough. The public library is finding that it is helpful to create opportunities for young people not only by helping them to gain Internet access, but by empowering them by teaching them access skills. Enoch Pratt Free Library's "A Whole New World," implemented in 1995, targets and trains young people to master information access on the Internet. "Scooter," the running computer, serves as the project's mascot. Trained volunteers tutor students in approximately six one-on-one sessions of intensive skill-building workbook activities. The activities include learning about the computer, e-mail, and netiquette (see Appendix).

Trainees receive their "student driver's" permits (a photo identification card) and free e-mail accounts, and they take a pretest to determine what they know about computer use and accessing electronic data. The program aims to teach safe and responsible use of the Internet as well

> "While some exciting new things have been tried many of the best ideas are either borrowed or old . . . Look to our colleagues for good ideas, whether they be tried-and-true or wildly innovative."[6]
> —Stephen Del Vecchio (Director of the DeWitt Wallace – Reader's Digest CLASP

as to create a sense of adventure and confidence in the use of technology. Students complete a posttest that measures what they have learned and receive certificates of completion. We use a volunteer manual for quality control and to increase the comfort levels for many of the trainers. This test drive of the Internet helps young people to understand how to use the technology for information and recreation. They also learn what an integral role the library plays in bringing the technology to them.

REFERENCES

1. Lowell Martin, *Baltimore Reaches Out: Library Service to the Disadvantaged* (Baltimore, MD: Enoch Pratt Library, 1967).
2. Discussed in Stan Weisner, *Information Is Empowering: Developing Public Library Sevices for Youth At-Risk* (Oakland, GRT, 1992).
3. Mary K. Chelton, ed., *Excellence in Library Services to Young Adults* (Chicago: American Library Association, 1994), 10.
4. "Aladdin's Theme," Wonderland Music Co., Inc., 1992.
5. Ernest Imhoff, "Foundation Aims to Bring Commitment to Action Here," *The Sun*, (17 Jan. 1996), 3B.
6. Stephen Del Vecchio, "School and Public Library Corporation: Connecting Libraries and Schools with CLASP," *Wilson Library Bulletin* (1993): 40.

Bibliography

1999 Kids Count Data Online. Available <http//:www.kidscount.org/kidscount/kc1999/>. Accessed 5/8/00.

Adess, Nancy, Erika Jenssen, and Carolyn Lieber. *"Bay Area Library & Information Systems (BALIS) Needs Assessment Report, Richmond, and San Pablo."* 1991 Report.

Annie Casey Foundation. *Kids Count Data Book: State Profiles of Well-Being.* Baltimore: The Foundation, 1994.

———. "Kids Count Special Report: When Teens Have Sex: Issues and Trends." Baltimore: The Foundation, 1998.

———. "New Futures: The Path of Most Resistance: Reflections on Lessons Learned from New Futures." Baltimore: The Foundation, 1995.

Anson, Amy R. et al. "The Comer School Development Program: A Theoretical Analysis," *Urban Education,* 26 (Apr. 1991): 56–82.

Auletta, Ken. *The Underclass.* New York: Random House, 1982.

Ball, Jerry, Marie Hunter, and Judy Porta. "Bay Area Library and Information System (BALIS) Youth-At-Risk Project, Livermore." 1991 Report.

Barnes, Miranda. "Program Opens Doors to a Whole New World," *The Sun*, 11 Mar. 1996, A3, 2.

Bauer, David G. *The "How-To" Grants Manual: Successful Grantseeking Techniques for Obtaining Public and Private Grants, 2d ed.* New York: Oryx, 1993.

Beels, Jessica. *Kids Voices Count: Illuminating the Statistics.* Washington, DC: Children's Express, 1994.

Bode, Janet. *Stories of the Unexpected Achievers: Beating the Odds.* New York: Franklin Watts, 1991.

Branden, Nathaniel. *How to Raise Your Self-Esteem.* New York: Bantam Books, 1987.

Carnegie Council on Adolescent Development, Task Force on Education of Young Adolescents. *Turning Points: Preparing American Youth for the 21st Century.* New York: Carnegie Corporation of New York, 1989.

Chelton, Mary K., ed. *Excellence in Library Services to Young Adults.* Chicago: American Library Association, 1994.

Cherry, Charles. *Excellence without Excuse: The Black Student's Guide to Academic Excellence.* Fort Lauderdale, FL: International Scholastic Press, 1993.

Childers, Thomas A., and Nancy A. Van House. *What's Good? Describing Your Public Library's Effectiveness.* Chicago: American Library Association, 1993.

Clark, Terry A. "Evaluation: The Key to Reflective Management of School Reform for At-Risk Students," *Urban Education,* 26 (Apr. 1991): 43–55.

Clifton, Robert L., and Alan M. Dahms. *Grassroots Organizations: A Resource Book for Directors, Staff, and Volunteers of Small, Community-Based, Non-Profit Agencies,* 2d. ed. Prospect Heights, IL: Waveland, 1993.

Collins, Marva and Civias Tamarkin. *Marva Collins' Way.* Los Angeles: J.P. Tarcher, 1982.

Conner, Marlene. *What Is Cool? Understanding Black Manhood in America.* New York: Crown, 1995.

Conrad, Dan and Diane Hedin. *Youth Service: A Guidebook for Developing and Operating Effective Programs.* Washington, DC: Independent Sector, 1987.

Coplan, Kate, and Edwin Castagna, eds. *The Library Reaches Out.* New York: Oceana, 1965.

Council of Chief State School Officers. *Turning Points, States in Action: An Interim Report of the Middle Grade School State Policy Initiative.* Washington, DC: Resource Center on Educational Equity, 1992.

Council on Adolescent Development. *A Matter of Time: Risk and Opportunity in the Non-School Hours.* New York: Carnegie Corporation of New York, 1992.

Del Vecchio, Stephen. "School and Public Library Cooperation: Connecting Libraries with CLASP." *Wilson Library Bulletin,* (Sept, 1993): 38–40.

Delpit, Lisa. *Other People's Children: Cultural Conflict in the Classroom.* New York: The New Press, 1995.

Dryfoos, Joy. *Adolescents At-Risk: Prevalence and Prevention.* New York: Oxford University Press, 1990.

———. "School-Based Social and Health Services for At-Risk Students," *Urban Education,* 26 (Apr. 1991): 118–37.

Duncan, Claude, Douglas Rivlin, and Maggie Williams. "An Advocates Guide to the Media." Washington, DC: Children's Defense Fund, 1990.

Edelman, Peter, and Joyce Lander, eds. *Adolescence and Poverty: Challenge for the 1990s.* Washington, DC: Center for National Policy Press, 1991.

Edwards, Margaret A. *The Fair Garden and Swarm of Beasts: The Library and the Young Adult.* New York: Hawthorn Books, 1969.

Erickson, Judith B. *Directory of American Youth Organizations.* Minneapolis: Free Spirit, 1996.

Evans, Thomas W. *Mentoring: Making a Difference in Our Public Schools.* Princeton: Peterson's Guide, 1992.

FedStats. Available<http:www.fedstats.gov/>. Accessed 5/8/00.

Freedom, Marc. "The Kindness of Strangers: Reflections on the Mentoring Movement." Philadelphia: Public/Private Ventures, 1991.

Fremon, Celeste. *Father Greg and the Homeboys.* New York: Hyperion, 1995.

Geever, Jane C., and Patricia McNeill. *Guide to Proposal Writing.* New York: The Foundation Center, 1993.

General Colin Powell: "Opening Remarks" November 25, 1997. Available <http://www.americaspromise.org/NEAa.htm> Accessed 4/28/00.

Haberman, Martin, and William H. Richards. "Urban Teachers Who Quit: Why They Leave and What To Do," *Urban Education,* 25 (Oct. 1990): 297–303.

Hacker, Andrew. *Two Nations: Black and White, Separate, Hostile, Unequal.* New York: Charles Scribner's Sons, 1992.

Hale, Janice E. *Unbank the Fire: Visions for the Education of African American Children.* Baltimore: Johns Hopkins University Press, 1994.

Hamburg, David. *Today's Children: Creating a Future for a Generation in Crisis.* New York: Random House, 1992.

Hatkoff, Amy, and Karen Kelly Klopp. *How to Save the Children: An Innovative Resource Guide Filled with Practical Ideas to Counter the Effects of Poverty and Neglect on America's Children.* New York: Simon and Schuster, 1992.

Hillman, Howard, and Karin Abarbanel. *The Art of Winning Foundation Grants.* New York: Vanguard Press, 1975.

Himmel, Ethel E., and William James Wilson. *Planning for Results: A Public Library Transformation Process.* Chicago: American Library Association, 1998.

Imhoff, Ernest F. "Foundation Aims to Bring Commitment to Action Here," *The Sun,* 17 Jan. 1996, B3.

————. "Wanted: Aid Programs in the U.S.—That Succeed," *The Sun*, 12 Aug. 1996, B10.

"Information Is Empowering, Bay Area Youth-At-Risk Project, Addendum Two: Nine Youth-At-Risk Services Plans. 1991 Report.

Jones, Patrick. *Connecting Young Adults and Libraries: A How-To-Do-It Manual*, 2d ed. New York: Neal Schuman, 1998.

Katznelson, Ira, and Margaret Weir. *The Decline of the Democratic Ideal*. New York: Basic Book, 1985.

Kaywell, Joan F. *Adolescents at Risk: A Guide to Fiction and Nonfiction for Young Adults, Parents, and Professionals*. Westport, CT: Greenwood, 1993.

Kiritz, Norton. "Program Planning & Proposal Writing." Los Angeles: Grantsmanship Center, 1979.

Kozol, Jonathan. *Savage Inequalities: Children in America's Schools*. New York: Crown, 1991.

Kunjufu, Jawanza. *Developing Positive Self-Images and Discipline in Black Children*. Chicago: African American Image, 1984.

Kurzig, Carol M. *Foundation Fundamentals: A Guide For Grant Seekers*. New York: Foundation Center, 1981.

Lancaster, F. W. *If You Want to Evaluate Your Library*, 2d ed. Champaign: University of Illinois, Graduate School of Library Science, 1993.

Lent, Laura. "San Francisco Public Library Youth-At-Risk Program Proposal." 1991 Report.

Lewis, Catherine C. *Educating Hearts and Minds: Reflections on Japanese Preschool and Elementary Education*. New York: Press Syndicate of the University of Cambridge, 1995.

"Library in At-Risk Community Wins California Diversity Prize." *Library Hotline*, 25 no. 13 (1 Apr. 1996): 6–7.

Magid, Ken and Carole A. McKelvey. *High Risk Children without a Conscience*. Golden, CO: M&M Publishing, 1987.

Mathews, Virginia H., ed. *Library Services for Children and Youth: Dollars and Sense*. New York: Neal-Schuman, 1994.

McClenahan, Carolyn. *Teen Troubles: How to Keep Them from Becoming Tragedies*. New York: Walker, 1988.

McClure, Charles R., et al. *Planning and Roles Setting for Public Libraries: A Manual of Options and Procedures*. Chicago: American Library Association, 1987.

McLaughlin, Mibrey, Merita A. Irby, and Juliet Langman. *Urban Sanctuaries: Neighborhood Organizations in the Lives and Future of Inner-City Youth*. San Francisco: Jossey-Bass, 1994.

Mincy, Ronald, ed. *Nurturing Young Black Males: Challenges to Agencies, Programs and Social Policy*. Washington, DC: The Urban Institute, 1994.

Newberg, Norman A. "Contexts That Promote Success for Inner-City Students," *Urban Education*, 31 (May 1996): 149–76.

Nielson, Linda. *How to Motivate Adolescents: A Guide for Parents, Teachers, and Counselors*. New York: Prentice Hall, 1982.

Nyren, Dorothy, comp., ed. *Community Service: Innovations in Outreach at the Brooklyn Public Library*. Chicago: 1970. American Library Association, 1970.

Office of Educational Research and Improvement, U.S. Department of Education, Youth Indicators 1991: Trends in the Well-Being of America's Youth.Washington, DC: U.S. DOE, 1991.

Paley, Vivian Gussin. *Kwanzaa and Me: A Teacher's Story*. Cambridge: Harvard University Press, 1995.

Payne, Charles. "The Comer Intervention Model and School Reform in Chicago, Implications of Two Models of Change." *Urban Education*, 26 (Apr. 1991): 8–24.

Peterson, Kenneth D., Betsy Bennett, and Douglas F. Sherman. "Themes of Uncommonly Successful Teachers of At-Risk Students," *Urban Education*, 26 (Jul. 1991): 176–94.

Polonio, Narcisca, and Ronald Williams. "The Politics of Funding At-Risk Programs in the 1990s," *Urban Education*, 26 (Apr. 1991): 43–55.

Prowthow-Stith, D. *Deadly Consequences: How Violence Is Destroying Our Teenage Population and a Plan to Begin Solving the Problems*. New York: Harper Collins, 1991.

Roehlkepartain, Eugene C. "Reaching the Underserved." *Source*, 11, no. 1 (April, 1995): 1–5.

Ross, Roberta. "An Advocate's Guide to Fund Raising." Washington, DC: The Children's Defense Fund, 1990.

Schneiter, Paul H. *The Art of Asking: How to Solicit Philanthropic Gifts, 2d ed.* Maryland: Fundraising Institute, 1985.

Shavit, David. "The Distribution of Public Library Services." *Public Library Quarterly* 5 (Summer 1984): 59–68.

Simons, Jane, and Donna Jabolonski. "An Advocate's Guide to Using Data." Washington, DC: The Children's Defense Fund, 1990.

Smith, Gregory. "Essays, Reviews: The Challenge to Care In Schools," *Urban Education*, 29 (Apr. 1994): 104–24.

Smulyan, Marilyn. "San Francisco Youth-At-Risk Needs Assessment Project." 1991 Report.

Steele, Victoria, and Stephen D. Elder. *Becoming a Fundraiser: The Prin-*

ciples and Practice of Library Development. Chicago: America Library Association, 1992.

Stevenson, John O. "Tales of Risk, of Deliverance, and the Redemption of Learning," *Urban Education,* 26 (Apr. 1991): 94–104.

Talkington, Audrey E. and Barbara Albers-Hill. *To Save a Child: Things You Can Do to Protect, Nurture and Teach Our Children.* New York: Avery, 1993.

Trachtman, Roberta. "Early Childhood Education and Child Care: Issues of At-Risk Children and Families." *Urban Education,* 26 (Apr. 1991): 25–42.

Van House, Nancy A., and Thomas Childers. "Prospects for Public Library Evaluation," *Public Libraries,* 30 (Sept./Oct. 1991): 274–78.

Viadero, Debra. "Against All Odds: Why Do Some Children Succeed in the Face of Adversity While Others—Growing Up in the Same Circumstances Fail?" *Teacher Magazine,* 7 (May/June 1995): 20–22.

Walter, Virginia A. *Output Measures and More Planning and Evaluating Public Library Services for Young Adults.* Chicago: American Library Association, 1995.

Weisner, Stan. *Conference Guidebook for Developing Library Services for Youth-At-Risk.* Oakland: GRT, 1992.

———. *Information Is Empowering: Developing Public Library Services for Youth At-Risk.* Oakland: GRT, 1992.

Willits, Arlene. *Alameda Free Library Youth-At-Risk Needs Assessment Report.* 1991.

Appendix

Organizations That Serve Youth

Many of the organizations listed below represent collaborative opportunities for libraries to serve at-risk youth on a variety of levels. The list includes those organizations that young people may join, those that make public policy and disseminate information, and those that provide grants. In addition, several of these national organizations have local branches.

Membership for Youth

ASPIRA Association, Inc

1112 16th St., NW, Ste. 340, Washington, DC 20036, (202) 835-3600
<www.aspira.org>

Headquartered in Washington, D.C., this organization focuses on the promotion of education and leadership among Hispanic youth. There are several affiliates in communities located in Florida, Illinois, New Jersey, New York, Connecticut, and Puerto Rico. Young people who participate in ASPIRA Clubs develop leadership and academic skills, work in the community, and learn about careers. Most participants are from low-income families.

BIG BROTHERS/BIG SISTERS OF AMERICA

230 North 13th St., Philadelphia, PA 19107, (215) 567-7000
<www.bbsa.org>

This national organization with 500 local agencies pairs children and adults one-on-one. The adults serve as friends, mentors, and role models. In an effort to fulfill its commitment to reach more at-risk youth, Big Brothers/Big Sisters seeks to recruit

Minority volunteers, work with schools, and train, and involve older adults as mentors.

BOYS AND GIRLS CLUBS OF AMERICA

1230 W. Peachtree St. NW, Atlanta, GA 30309-4447, (404) 815-5778
<www.bgca.org>

This national federated organization consists of local independent clubs throughout the United States. The major focus of their program centers on activities designed to teach good work habits, teamwork, perseverance, self-reliance, and consideration of others. Boys and Girls Clubs of America has implemented strategies to attract and serve more at-risk youth, especially those living in public housing.

BOY SCOUTS OF AMERICA

1325 W. Walnut Hill Lane, P.O. Box 152079, Irving TX 75015, (972) 580-2000
<www.bsa.scouting.org>

Founded in 1910, this national organization strives to build character, foster citizenship, and enhance mental, moral, and physical fitness in young people within the context of fun, adventure, and education. Boy Scouts of America has designed several programs to reach at-risk youth in both rural and urban communities.

CAMP FIRE BOYS AND GIRLS

4601 Madison Ave., Kansas City, MO 64112, (816) 756-0258
<www.campfire.org>

Self-development, skill development, and social development are the major focuses of this national organization. Camp Fire Boys and Girls has made reaching more at-risk youth a national priority.

GIRL SCOUTS OF THE U.S.A.

420 Fifth Ave., New York, NY 10018-2202, (212) 852-8000
<www.gsusa.org>

Founded in 1912, this organization supports the educational growth and development of girls aged five to seventeen. They provide opportunities for girls to have experiences that assist them with decision making and self-awareness. Skill-building activities address personal well being and fitness; new learning technologies; and awareness of other cultures. In recent years, the organization's outreach efforts have included diversifying membership to include a greater racial, ethnic, and economic balance.

GIRLS INCORPORATED

30 East 33rd St., New York, NY 10016, (212) 689-3700
<www.girlsinc.org>

Girls Incorporated is dedicated to helping girls build self-esteem and independence, and develop skills that allow them to recognize their potential. The organization has introduced several initiatives that address at-risk behavior.

JUNIOR ACHIEVEMENT, INC.

1 Education Way, Colorado Springs, CO 80906-4477, (719) 540-8000
<www.ja.org>

This national organization with local franchises teaches economic and business concepts to young people in grades K-12. Junior Achievement's outreach initiatives include "Success Now," a program to aid students in making the transition from school to work, and the "the Economics of Staying in School," a school dropout prevention program in partnership with the National Urban League.

NATIONAL ASSOCIATION FOR THE ADVANCEMENT OF COLORED PEOPLE (NAACP)

4805 Mt. Hope Drive, Baltimore, MD 21215, (410) 358-8900
<www.naacp.org>

This organization was founded in 1909, in part to eliminate racial prejudice through non-violence. In 1935, the NAACP established its Youth and College Division in an effort to aid youth in their development of leadership and citizenship skills. Several years ago, the organization developed initiatives to reach less advantaged and underserved at-risk youth through tutoring, counseling, and school dropout prevention programs.

NATIONAL 4-H CLUBS

7100 Connecticut Avenue, Chevy Chase, MD 20815, (301) 962-2820
<www.fourhcouncil.edu>

This organization has begun to focus more on youth-at-risk initiatives
that reach underserved groups. Founded in 1914 as part of the U.S. Department of Agriculture's Cooperative Extension Service, the National
4-H Clubs provide hands-on projects that stimulate the development of
life skills.

NATIONAL URBAN LEAGUE

120 Wall St., New York, NY 10005, (212) 558-5300
<www.nul.org>

The mission of the National Urban League is to help African Americans gain social and economic equality and to promote equal opportunity for African Americans, other minorities, and the poor. After making
youth services a national priority in 1991, the League launched a club
based program titled NULITES (National Urban League Incentives to
Excel and Succeed). NULITES aims to improve academic achievement
among African-American students ages twelve to eighteen.

YMCA OF THE USA

101 North Wacker Drive, Chicago, IL 60606-7386, (312) 997-0031
<www.ymca.com>

Many local branches of the YMCA offer programs that support the health
and social service needs of at-risk youth. YMCA initiatives focus on building self-esteem, improving personal health, and developing employment
skills and career goals.

YWCA OF THE USA

350 Fifth Avenue, Ste. 301, New York, NY 10118, (212) 273-7800
<www.ywca.org>

Founded in 1858, local branches of the YWCA of the U.S.A. currently
offer classes, workshops, and seminars that promote health, well-being
and personal development mainly for young women. Feature programs
include health instruction, teen pregnancy prevention, family life education, self-esteem enhancement, parenting, and career exploration.

Public Policy/Disseminates Information

AMERICA'S PROMISE THE ALLIANCE FOR YOUTH

909 North Washington Street, Ste. 400, Alexandria, VA 22314-1556, (703) 535-3900 <www.americaspromise.org>

This organization coordinates initiatives of numerous organizations to ensure that millions of at-risk youth develop marketable skills, and live in a safe and healthy environment with caring, responsible adults. In addition, they promote collaborative efforts among community groups through the "Communities of Promise" initiative.

THE BUREAU FOR AT-RISK YOUTH

135 Dupont St., P.O. Box 760, Plainview, NY 11803-0760, 1 (800) 999-6884 < www.at-risk.com>

Founded in 1990, the Bureau publishes and distributes a wide range of innovative products used by educators, counselors, parents, and young people. They publish a quarterly catalog, "At-Risk Resources."

CENTER FOR HUMAN RESOURCES

Florence Heller Graduate School, Brandies University, 60 Turner Street, Waltham, MA 02154, (617) 736-3770 <www.brandeis.edu/heller>

This research, training, and policy development organization strives to connect scholarly youth development research and practical work with youth experiences in ways to benefit administrators and practitioners. The Center for Human Resources' efforts help to address issues of quality of life for low-income youth and their families

CENTER FOR YOUTH DEVELOPMENT AND POLICY RESEARCH

Academy for Educational Development, 1875 Connecticut Ave., NW, Washington, DC 20009-1202, (202) 884-8400 <www.aed.org>

Center for Youth Development and Policy Research conducts youth research and policy analyses, provides information about outstanding youth programs, polices, and promotes dialogue and sharing among youth-serving groups. The organization also implements program evaluations, community assessments, and a variety of youth demonstration projects. The center strives to enhance the future for at-risk children and youth.

CENTER FOR YOUTH STUDIES

130 Essex St., South Hamilton, MA 01982, (978) 646-4066
<www.centerforyouth.org>

This center publishes the useful *Encyclopedia of Youth Services*, a computerized information database about teens. Topics include trends, attitudes, hopes, and fears.

CHILD WELFARE LEAGUE OF AMERICA

440 First St., NW Washington, DC 20001, (202) 638-2952
<www.cwla.com>

This organization established in 1920 is dedicated solely to assisting at-risk children and their families. The League is comprised of several hundred local public and private child welfare agencies that provide support a large percentage of single-parent and low-income families. On a national level CWLA serves as an advocate for children and their families through developing standards, distributing research findings, consulting, and so on.

NATIONAL BLACK CHILD DEVELOPMENT INSTITUTE

1023 15th St., NW Suite 600, Washington, DC, 20005, (202) 387-1281
<www.nbcdi.org>

This institute, founded in 1970, strives to improve the quality of life for African American children and youth. The Institute seeks to inform communities about national, state, and local issues affecting children and youth in four main areas: education, child care/early childhood education, child welfare, and health. In addition, it trains people to better serve African American children and youth.

NATIONAL COALITION OF HISPANIC HEALTH AND HUMAN SERVICES ORGANIZATIONS (COSSMHO)

1501 16th St., NW, Washington, DC 20036, (202) 387-5000
<www.cossmho.org>

This membership organization of individuals, community organizations, national organizations, and educational institutions dedicates it efforts toward improving community-based health and human services for Hispanics. COSSMHO programs for at-risk youth include peer counseling, teen theater, and family intervention. COSSMHO also publishes books and videos relative to adolescent concerns.

NATIONAL NETWORK FOR YOUTH

1319 F St., NW, Ste. 401, Washington, DC 20004, (202) 783-7949
<www.nn4youth.org>

Representing hundreds of agencies that serve runaway, homeless, and other youth in high-risk situations, the National Network for Youth seeks to empower youth, strengthen families, and encourage healthy alternatives for youth. The organization promotes model programs, serves as a resource for information on shelters and agencies, and provides effective intervention strategies and service delivery. Its web site, YouthNet, connects teens and service providers to critical information about young people.

Provides Grants

ANNIE E. CASEY FOUNDATION

701 St. Paul St., Baltimore, MD 21202, (410) 547-6600
<www.aecf.org>

Located in Baltimore, Maryland, The Annie E. Casey Foundation, is a national institution dedicated exclusively to improving the lives of disadvantaged children and families. The foundation provides millions of dollars in grant money in support of programs that benefit at-risk youth. They publish the *Kids Count Data Book*.

INTERNATIONAL YOUTH FOUNDATION

32 South St., Ste. 500, Baltimore, MD 21202, (410) 347-1500)
<www.iyfnet.org>

Founded in 1990, the International Youth Foundation provides support worldwide to offer foundations that assist groups that address global issues such as drug and alcohol use, violence, teen pregnancy, school dropouts, etc. IYF has networked with foundations in countries around the world including Poland, Germany, Slovakia, Ireland, Ecuador, the Philippines, Thailand, and South Africa.

Index

About the Author

JoAnn Mondowney has over 25 years of librarianship rooted in service to young adults. Her active and long term service in support of young people in the Young Adult Library Services Association, a division of the American Library Association, includes program planning, strategic long-range planning, and budget and finance. She has experience as a branch manager and administrator at the Enoch Pratt Free Library—nationally known for its commitment to excellence and innovation in serving young adults. She is the creator of the nationally aclaimed electronic literacy at-risk project "A Whole New World."